The Living Flame of Love

by St. John of the Cross
with His Letters, Poems,
and Minor Writings

Syida ll. long
2727 Hilbert Street
San francisco, CA 94123

The Living Flame of Love

by St. John of the Cross
with His Letters, Poems,
and Minor Writings

ST. JOHN OF THE CROSS

AND DAVID LEWIS, TRANSLATOR

COSIMOCLASSICS

NEW YORK

**The Living Flame of Love by St. John of the Cross
with His Letters, Poems, and Minor Writings**
Cover © 2007 Cosimo, Inc.

For information, address:

Cosimo, P.O. Box 416
Old Chelsea Station
New York, NY 10113-0416

or visit our website at:
www.cosimobooks.com

*The Living Flame of Love by St. John of the Cross with His Letters, Poems,
and Minor Writings* was originally published in 1912.

Cover design by www.kerndesign.net

ISBN: 978-1-60206-429-4

O Living Flame of Love,
That woundest tenderly
My soul in its inmost depth!
As thou art no longer grievous,
Perfect thy work, if it be thy will,
Break the web of this sweet encounter.

—from *The Living Flame of Love*

CONTENTS

THE LIVING FLAME OF LOVE

AN ESSAY ON ST. JOHN OF THE CROSS

WRITTEN BY HIS EMINENCE CARDINAL WISEMAN
AS A PREFACE TO THE FIRST ENGLISH EDITION

IT is now many years ago, long before the episcopal burthen pressed upon his shoulders, that the author enjoyed the pleasure of knowing, and frequently conversing with, the estimable Görres at Munich. One day the conversation turned on a remark in that deep writer's *Philosophy of Mysticism*, to the effect that saints most remarkable for their mystical learning and piety were far from exhibiting, in their features and expression, the characteristics usually attributed to them. They are popularly considered, and by artists represented, as soft, fainting, and perhaps hysterical persons ; whereas their portraits present to us countenances of men, or women, of a practical, business-like, working character.

The author asked Görres if he had ever seen an original likeness of St. Teresa, in whom he had thought these remarks were particularly exemplified. He replied that he never had ; and the writer, on returning to Rome, fulfilled the promise

which he had made the philosopher, by procuring
a sketch of an authentic portrait of that saint,
preserved with great care in the Monastery of St.
Sylvester, near Tusculum. It was painted for
Philip II. by a concealed artist, while he was
conversing with her.

This portrait confirms most strongly the theory
of Görres, as the author wrote to him with the
drawing ; for while no mystical saint has ever
been more idealised by artists, or represented as
living in a continual swoon, than St. Teresa, her
true portraits all represent her with strong,
firmly set, and almost masculine features, with
forms and lines that denoted vigour, resolution,
and strong sense. Her handwriting perfectly
suggests the same conclusion.

Still more does the successful activity of her
life, in her many painful struggles, under every
possible disadvantage, and her final and complete
triumph, strengthen this idea of her. And then,
her almost superhuman prudence, by which she
guided so many minds, and prosperously conducted so many complicated interests and affairs,
and her wonderful influence over men of high
education and position, and of great powers, are
further evidences of her strong, commanding
nature ; such as, in the world, might have claimed
an almost unexampled pre-eminence.

It is not improbable that some who take up

these volumes, or dip into them here and there, may conceive that they were written by a dreamy ascetic, who passed his life in hazy contemplation of things unreal and unpractical. Yet it was quite the contrary. Twin-saint, it may be said, to St. Teresa—sharer in her labours and in her sufferings, St. John of the Cross, actively and unflinchingly pursued their joint object, that of reforming and restoring to its primitive purity and observance the religious Order of Carmelites, and founding, throughout Spain, a severer branch, known as discalced, or barefooted Carmelites ; or more briefly, as Teresians.

We do not possess any autobiography of St. John, as we do of St. Teresa, or the more active portion and character of his life would be at once apparent. Moreover, only very few of his letters have been preserved—not twenty, in fact—or we should undoubtedly have had sufficient evidence of his busy and active life. But, even as it is, proofs glance out from his epistles of this important element in his composition.

In his [third] letter he thus writes to the religious of Veas, a highly favoured foundation : 'What is wanting in you, if, indeed, anything be wanting, is . . . silence and work. For, whereas speaking distracts, silence and action collect the thoughts and strengthen the spirit.' And again : ' To arrest this evil, and to preserve our spirit, as I have said, there is no surer remedy than to suffer, to work, to be silent.'

It was not, therefore, a life of visionary or speculative meditation that St. John taught even the nuns to pursue, but one of activity and operative occupation. But we may judge of his own practice by a passage in another of his letters. Thus he writes :

' I have been waiting to finish these visitations and foundations which our Lord has hastened forward in such wise that there has been no time to spare. The friars have been received at Cordova with the greatest joy and solemnity on the part of the whole city. . . . I am now busied at Seville with the removal of the nuns, who have bought one of the principal houses at a cost of about 14,000 ducats, being worth more than 20,000. They are now established there. Before my departure I intend to establish another house of friars here, so that there will be two of our Order in Seville. Before the feast of St. John, I shall set forth to Ecija, where, with the Divine blessing, we shall found another ; thence to Malaga. . . . I wish I had authority to make this foundation, as I had for the other. I do not expect much difficulty ' * (Letter VII).

---

* The writer has had the pleasure of visiting these early foundations at Seville, Ecija, Malaga, and Granada. The first fervour of the Order yet remains in them.

This is only a few months' work, or rather some weeks'; for the interval described in the letter is from the Ascension to the 24th of June. We must allow some portion of this time for the slow travelling of those days and those regions, over *sierras*, on muleback. And then, St. John's travels were not triumphal progresses, but often were painful pilgrimages, crossed by arrests, and even long imprisonments, embittered by personal unkindness.

Yet with calm firmness he persevered and travelled and worked at the establishment of his new houses in many parts of Spain, till the Order was fully and permanently planted. In fact, if we look only at his life, we should naturally conclude that he was a man of an operative mind, always at work, ever in movement, who could not afford much time for inward concentration on abstract subjects.

But when we read his writings, another high quality, for which we are not prepared, must strike us forcibly as entering into the composition of his character. He must have given much time to reading and study. He is learned in all those pursuits which we desire and expect to find in an ecclesiastical scholar of his age. Every page in his book gives proof of thorough acquaintance with that mental discipline which trained and formed the mind in the schools, and gave a mould into which thought ran and settled itself in fixed principles ; or, where this possessed extraordinary power, opened a channel through which it passed to further spheres of activity. Even the mind of a Bacon was conducted through the dialectics of those schools to all the developments of his intellectual vigour.

In St. John we discover, at every turn, a mind so educated by reading and by study. His writings are far from being a string of loose, disjointed thoughts, scattered apophthegms, or aimless rhapsodies. Quite on the contrary, there is ever a sequence and strict logical continuity in every division of his discourse, and all the several parts are coherent and consistent. However detailed his treatment of his subject, he never becomes entangled or confused ; he never drops a thread of what may appear a fine-spun web of expansion in a difficult topic, and loses it ; but he returns to what he has interrupted or intercalated with undisturbed fidelity, and repursues his reasoning with a distinctness and discrimination which shows that, in truth, there had been no interruption, but that unity of thought had pervaded all the design, and nothing had been left to chance or the idea of the moment.

Indeed, one feels in reading him that he has to deal with the master of a science. There is no wandering from the first purpose, no straying aside from the pre-determined road, after even flowers that grow on its sides. Every division and subdivision of the way has been charted from the beginning by one who saw it all before him. And the secret lies in this, and nothing more : St. John invents nothing, borrows nothing from others, but gives us clearly the results of his own experience in himself and in others. He presents you with a portrait, not with a fancy picture. He represents the ideal of one who has passed, as he had done, through the career of the spiritual life, through its struggles and its victories.

Not only does he at all times exhibit proof of his mental cultivation by those processes which formed every great mind in those days, and the gradual decline of which, in later times, has led proportionably to looseness of reasoning and diminution of thinking power, but St. John throughout exhibits tokens of a personal culture of his own mental powers and many graceful gifts.

His mind is eminently poetical, imaginative, tender, and gentle. Whatever mystical theology may appear to the mind of the uninitiated, to St. John it was clearly a bright and well-loved pursuit ; it was a work of the heart more than of the head ; its place was rather in the affections than among the intellectual powers. Hence, with every rigour of logical precision and an unbending exactness in his reasonings, there is blended a buoyancy of feeling, a richness of varied illustration, and often a sweet and elegant fancy playing with grave subjects, so as to render them attractive, which show a mind unfettered by mere formal methods, but easy in its movements and free in its flights. Indeed, often a point which is obscure and abstruse, when barely treated, receives, from a lively illustration, a clearness and almost brilliancy quite unexpected.

But the prominent learning of the saint, and the source of his most numerous and happiest elucidations, are to be found in the inspired Word of God. That is his treasure-house, that the inspirer of his wisdom and subject of his meditation. The sacred volume must have been in his hands all day, and can hardly have dropped out of them at night. Even by merely glancing at the index of texts quoted by him, placed at the end of [each] volume, any one may convince himself of his rare familiarity with the inspired writings, and one very different from what we may find among readers of Scripture in our days.

For, first, it is an impartial familiarity, not confined to some favourite portions as is often the case, where the reader thinks he finds passages or subjects that confirm his own views or encourage his tastes. But in St. John we discover

nothing of this sort. Of course, such a book as
the Canticle, the special food of mystics, is familiar
to his pen as it was to the mouths of Jewish
maidens, made sweeter and sweeter by frequent
reiterations. But every other book is almost
equally ready to his hand, to prove more formally,
occasionally illustrate, every one of his proposi-
tions. For the first purpose he must have deeply
studied the sacred text ; for the second, its
expressions must have been his very household
words.

Then, secondly, the beauty and elegance of his
applications prove not mere familiarity, but a
refined study and a loving meditation on what
he considers most holy and divine. Some of his
quotations are richly set in his graceful explanations and commentaries ; and though the adapta-
tions which he makes sometimes appear startling
and original to an ordinary peruser of Scripture,
they seem so apt and so profound in their spiritual
wisdom that they often win approbation and even
admiration.

So far it may appear that this Preface has dealt
with St. John of the Cross outside of the sphere
in which the volume to which it is prefixed represents him as moving. It has not treated him as
a mystical theologian. Why is this ? it may be
justly asked.

The answer must be honest and straight-

b

forward. It is too common for overlooking or disguising, to pronounce a contemplative life to be only a cloak for idleness, a pretext for abandoning or neglecting the active duties of domestic or social existence, and shrinking from their responsibilities. Those who profess to lead it are considered as the drones of the human hive, who leave its work to others and yet exact a share of its sweets. And if, from time to time, one emerges from the passive, or, as it is deemed, indolent condition of mere dreamers, and gives form and precision to the rules and laws which guide them, he is probably held merely to have more method and skill in his disordered ideas, and to be only more pernicious than his companions or followers.

This prejudice, firmly rooted in many English minds, it has been thought well to remove, as a preliminary to presenting St. John to his readers in his highest and distinctive character. He has been shown to possess other eminent qualities. He was a man of active life and practical abilities, industrious, conversant with business, where prudence, shrewdness, and calculation, as well as boldness, were required. He was a man of well-trained mind, cultivated by the exercise of intellectual faculties, and matured by solid, especially religious knowledge.

He has now to come before us as a diver into

the very depths of thought, as a contemplative of the highest order.

A man with such a character as we have claimed for him cannot have dozed away his years of life in unpractical dreams or in crude speculations. These would be incompatible with the rest of his character. His contemplativeness, and his mode of explaining it, may be anticipated to be methodical and practical, and at the same time feeling and attractive. And such both are his own practice and his communication of it to us.

But now, perhaps, many readers may ask for some introductory information on the very nature of the subjects treated in the volumes before him, and it cannot be reasonably refused. This may be conveyed in various ways ; perhaps the most simple and appreciable will be found in an analogy, though imperfect, with other spheres of thought.

It is well known that a mind naturally adapted to a pursuit, and thus led ardently to follow it, after having become thoroughly conversant and familiar with all its resources, becomes almost, or altogether, independent of its methods, and attains conclusions by compendious processes, or by intuitive foresight, which require in others long and often complicated deductions. Familiar illustrations may be found in our habitual speaking without thinking of our grammar, which a foreigner has constantly to do while learning our language ; or the almost inexplicable accuracy of calculation in even children gifted with the power of instantaneous arithmetical solutions.

A mathematician acquires by study this faculty ; and it is said that Laplace, in the decline of life, could not any longer fill up the gaps in the processes by which, at the age of greater mental vigour, he had reached, without effort, the most wonderful yet accurate conclusions.

What is to be found in these abstruser pursuits exists no less in those of a lighter character. The literary mind, whether in thinking, writing, or speaking, when well disposed by abilities and well tutored by application, takes in without effort the entire theme presented to it, even with its parts and its details. Sometimes it is like a landscape revealed, in a dark night, by one flash of lightning ; oftener it resembles the calmer contemplation of it, in bright day, by an artist's eye, which is so filled with its various beauties that it enables him to transfer it, at home, to the enduring canvas on which many may enjoy it.

The historian may see, in one glance, the exact plan of a work, with its specific aims and views ; its sources, too, and its auxiliary elucidations. The finished orator, no less, when suddenly called upon, will hold from end to end the drift and purpose of his entire discourse, and deliver, without effort, what to others appears an elaborate composition. But still more, the poet indulges in noblest flights up to the regions of sublime, or over the surface of beautiful, thoughts, while he appears to be engaged in ordinary occupation or momentarily musing in vague abstraction.

Indeed, even where manual action is required to give utterance to thought, the result is the same. The consummate musician sits down to a complicated instrument, silent and dumb till his fingers communicate to it his improvised imaginings ; bearing to its innermost organisation, by a sort of reflex action of the nerves of sensation on those of motion, the ready and inexhaustible workings of his brain, sweet melodies and rich harmonies, with tangled knots and delicious resolutions ; effortless, as if the soul were in the hand or the mechanical action in the head.

In the few examples which are here given, and which might easily be multiplied, the point illustrated is this : that where, with previous natural dispositions and persevering cultivation, perfection in any intellectual pursuit has been attained or approached, the faculty exercised in it becomes, in a manner, passive, dispenses with intermediate processes, and receives their ultimate conclusions stamped upon it. Labour almost ceases, and *spontaneity* of thought becomes its substitute.

In this condition of mind, familiar to any one

possessing genius in any form, perceptions, ideas, reasonings, imagery, have not to be sought ; they either dart at once complete into the thought, inborn and perfect to their very arms, as Pallas was symbolically fabled to express this process ; or they grow up, expanding from a small seed to a noble plant, but as if by an innate sap and vigour. There is a flow into the mind of un-sought images, or reflections, or truths ; whence they come, one hardly knows. They were not there before ; they have not been forged, or cast, or distilled within.

And when this spontaneous productiveness has been gained, the occupation of mind is not in-terrupted. St. Thomas is said to have concluded an argument against the Manichees alone at the royal table ; Bishop Walmesley renounced his mathematical studies on finding them painfully distract him at the altar. Neither recreation, nor serious employment, nor noise, nor any condi-tion of time or place, will suffice to dissipate or even to disturb the continuous, unlaborious, and unfatiguing absorption of thought in the mental region which has become its natural dwelling.

Let us now ask, Why may not a soul—that is, the mind accompanied by the best feelings—be placed in a similar position with relation to the noblest and sublimest object which it can pursue—GOD ?

He and His attributes present more perfect claims, motives and allurements, and more full gratification, repletion, and reward to earnest and affectionate contemplation, than any other object or subject. How much soever the mathematician may strain his intellect in pursuit of the true, however the poet may luxuriate in the enjoyment of the beautiful, to whatsoever extent the moralist may delight in the apprehension of the good in its recondite quintessence, none of these can reach, in his special aim and longing, that elevation and consummation which can be attained in those of all the three, by one whose contemplation is directed to the Infinite in Truth, in Beauty, and in Goodness.*

Why, then, should not this, so comprehensive and so grand a source of every mental enjoyment, become a supreme, all-exhausting, and sole object of contemplative fruition? Why should not some, or rather many, minds be found which have selected this as their occupation, their solace, their delight ; and found it to be what none other can of its nature be, inexhaustible? Everything else is measurable and fathomable ; this alone unlimited.

* It is recorded of the celebrated, though perhaps eccentric scholar, Raymund Lully, that once he entered the school of Duns Scotus, to whom he was unknown. The lecturer addressed to him the question, *Quotuplex pars scientiae est Deus ?*—'What part of knowledge includes God ?' His reply overmastered the interrogator : *Deus non est pars, qui est Totum*—'God is in no part—He is the WHOLE.'

Then, if there be no repugnance to such a choice being made in the aim of contemplation, it is natural for us to expect conditions and laws in its attainments analogous to what we find where the mental powers have selected for their exercise some inferior and more restricted object. There will be the same gradual and often slow course of assiduous training, the same difficulty of fixing and concentrating the thoughts ; till, by degrees, forms and intermediate steps are dispensed with ; when the mind becomes passive, and its trains of thought seem spontaneous and in-coming, rather than worked out by elaborating processes.

This state, when God is the sole occupier of thought, represents the highest condition of contemplation, the reaching of which Mystical Theology professes to direct.

There are, however, two essential differences between the natural and the spiritual exercises of the contemplative faculties. In treating of the first, a natural aptitude was named throughout as a condition for attaining that highest sphere of spontaneous suggestion in the mind. In the second, this condition is not included. Its place is taken by the supernatural power of GRACE.

Every believer in Christianity acknowledges the existence of an inward gift, which belongs of right to all; though many may not choose to claim it. It takes the place of mere natural advantages so completely, that its name has become a rooted word in our language, even apart from religion. We say that a man ' has had, or has not had, the grace ' to do a good thing; ' a graceless act ' is, in some way, evil; ' a grace-less youth ' is one walking, somehow, on the path leading to perdition. And we feel, and say, that it is grace which makes a poor man often more virtuous, and virtuously wise, though ignorant, and in other ways not wise-minded, than clever, better-educated, and more intellectual rich ones.

Whoever thus believes in a superhuman gift, which supplies, in the higher life of man, the ordinary powers of nature, or elevates these to the attainment of what requires more than ordinary qualities, will hardly be able to deny that this supernatural aid will be copiously granted, where the whole energy of a soul is directed exclusively to the most holy and sublime of purposes, the knowledge and contemplation of God. If it be easily accepted that any one reading, with pure and simple docility, His written records is helped by this grace to understand them, it surely is not much to ask, that one may expect no less assistance when, instead of the eye running over a written page, the entire soul is centred in Him, and every power, and every affection, is absorbed in deep and silent meditation on His own Divine essence.

A further distinction between the application of man's noblest faculties, combined to their simplest but sublimest possible object, and their separate exercise on any inferior speculation, consists in this. God, towards Whom the mystical contemplative directs himself, is a living, active Power, at once without and within the soul. Every Christian believes that He deals as such with the individual man ; that in his natural life each one has received his destiny, his time and place, and measure of both, by a special allotment ; that in his outward being, whatever befalls him, he is the ward of a personal Providence ; while in his inward and unseen existence he receives visitations of light, of remorse, of strength, and of guidance, which can apply and belong to him alone.

If so, how can he doubt that one of his own kind and class, who, more than tens of thousands, singles out that Giver of every good gift as supereminent, or rather sole claimant of his soul's best tributes ; the throne on which all his ideal conceptions of the great and the good are concentrated in a single unclouded vision of majesty and glory ; the altar on which are laid, in willing oblation, all his tenderest affections, and, in ready immolation, every inferior appetite and desire—who can doubt

that such a one establishes a right to a larger
share than others of the active interposition of
Divine kindness, and of personal favour in second-
ing his disinterested love ?

These two differences, great and essential,
show that we have been only illustrating, rather
than vindicating, the spiritual science of St.
John, by comparing it with other classes of
knowledge. We have endeavoured to prove that,
even prescinding from the spiritual quality, which
is its characteristic, there is nothing singular,
unnatural, or reprehensible in what would only
add one more, and a most worthy, mental pursuit
to those which generally receive not mere approbation but praise.

And hence the religious and ascetic contemplative may be allowed not only to deserve equal
admiration with the poet or philosopher, but to
be as fit as either for the ordinary duties of life,
and in as full possession of practical and social
virtues.

Having thus, by this analogy, disposed the
uninitiated reader to judge unprejudicedly of this
spiritual occupation of so many persons of sin-
gularly virtuous life in the Catholic Church,
we may invite him to consider if it have not
strong presumptions in its favour.

But, first, it may be well to give a brief explanation of this religious mysticism of which

the works of St. John are considered to treat so admirably. What we have already said will greatly assist us.

In the Catholic Church, besides public or private vocal prayer, every one is directed and urged to the practice of mental prayer, or meditation. For this duty the Church furnishes simple rules and methods, varying somewhat, but all with one practical end. She has at hand almost countless models, forms, and even fully developed drafts, scarcely requiring to be filled in.

In carrying out this familiar practice, it will be obvious that very different degrees of success will be attained. To some it continues, almost to the end, irksome and trying, full of distraction and imperfection. This may easily arise from natural deficiencies in the mind, or from habitual negligence. But to a willing and persevering mind these difficulties will diminish, and the power of concentrating the thoughts and affections upon a given subject will increase and strengthen.

Thus far any one may aspire, with every chance of success. Then comes a higher stage : when this power of fixing the mind is not only easy, but most pleasing ; when, without formal guidance, the soul rests, like the bird poised upon its wings, motionless above the earth, plunged, as it were, in the calm atmosphere which surrounds and sustains it on every side. This is the state of contemplation, when the placid action of a deeply inward thoughtfulness, undisturbed by other objects, is intent on gazing upon images and scenes fixed or passing as on a mirror before it, without exertion or fatigue, almost without note of time.

This condition, with its requisite power, is also attainable by those who regularly and seriously apply to meditation.* Yet, when we have reached it, we are still standing on the ground, and have not set foot on the first step of the ' mystical ladder ' which St. John teaches how to mount.

Far above the earthly exercise of contemplation is one which belongs to a much higher and purer sphere, above the clouds and mists of the one in which we move. To reach it is given to few ; and of those few, fewer still have left us records of their experience. Yet—and this is sufficient for our present purpose—that the consummation of their desires, and attainment of their scope, was a closer union with God, is acknowledged by all. The soul, thoroughly purified of all other affections, reaches a sublime and supernatural power of setting all its faculties in the contempla-

---

* Any one familiar with the Exercises of St. Ignatius will understand the difference between meditation and contemplation, in the sense here used ; and how from one he is led to the other. This is very different from the ' prayer of contemplation ' which belongs to mystical theology.

tion of the Supreme Being with such clearness and intensity, that its very existence seems lost in Him ; the most perfect conformity and uniformity with all the emanations of His will are established as its guiding laws ; and, as far as is yet compatible, union the most complete is obtained between the imperfect spirit of man and the infinite Spirit that created it to its own image and likeness.

Now, this aim of infirm humanity, and the possibility of reaching it, may appear, at first sight, extravagant and presumptuous. Yet there has hardly ever, if ever, existed a religious system which has not supposed such an aspiration as its highest, but still possible, flight to be within the reach of some more favoured votaries.

It is too well known to require proof that there existed, beyond a gross visible idolatry, a hidden, esoteric, and mysterious system in the mythologies of the East, handed down in the succession of their priesthoods. The mystic teachings of India, the best known to us, because we possess their works, reveal this doctrine to us, that contemplation is the means by which a man may attain to unification of himself with the Deity, rising by steps gradually to this almost blissful enjoyment of His presence. In China the sect or school of Lao-tseu, with which the learned Abel Rémusat made Europe acquainted by a special memoir, taught and practised the same mystical system.

Chaldea and Egypt no doubt held it also ; for it was from them that Pythagoras borrowed, and infused into the philosophy of Greece and Italy precisely the same doctrine ; for while his foolish theory, also Oriental, of transmigration put off to an indefinite period the fruition of the Divine essence, he taught that the soul, thoroughly purified and detached from every inferior affection, could, through contemplation, attain a union with God.

Although this sublime philosophy became obscured in the ages which succeeded him, it shone forth again in the Neoplatonic school—in Plotinus, Porphyrius and their followers. Whether they merely revived a faded, or published an occult, tradition of their heathen philosophy, or whether they were disfigured doctrines and practices from the still young and fresh Christianity of their times, it matters but little. In the one case we conclude how instinctive it is to man, even amidst absurd wanderings of his intellect, to expect, nay to crave for, not merely an approach to God, but unification with Him ; * and such a noble and holy desire and longing of humanity may naturally

* In races of both continents a ruder yet deeply symbolical feeling prevailed at all times, that incorporation with the Deity was obtained by partaking of the victims offered to Him. See Gerbet's beautiful treatise, *Sur le Dogme générateur de la Piété Catholique*.

expect to find satisfaction in the true revelation of man's Creator.

In the second hypothesis, we must admit that already Christianity had sufficiently developed the germs of its mystical system to be known to aliens, and even enemies.

Indeed, we cannot doubt that the religion of Christ, following the early manifestations of God in the Old Testament, laid deep those seeds of highest contemplation which were at once matured in His apostles. St. Paul, who was taken to the third heaven, to hear words unutterable to man and to require a severe counterpoise to the greatness of his revelations (2 Cor. xii.), came to be united with his Lord so as to hold but one life with and in Him (Gal. ii. 20 ; Phil. i. 21).

As to the existence, in the seers and holy sages of the Old Law, of a state of unitive contemplation, as in Abraham, Job, Moses, and Elias, we are not called aside to speak or consider. This point may be safely left in the hands of St. John of the Cross ; for though he does not anywhere expressly treat of this point, he has so filled his pages with quotations from every part of Scripture in illustration of his teaching, and the texts alleged by him are so apt and naturally applied, as to force conviction upon us that the mystical and spiritual communion with God was carried to the highest degree. Nay, does not a state of close intercommunion between God and man, through revelations, manifestations, angelic messages, and the prophetic spirit, on the one hand, and visions and ecstasies on the other, necessarily suppose it ? And does the frequent boldness of the Psalmist's familiarity with God, still more the domestic intimacy with Him so tenderly shadowed forth in the Canticle of Canticles, allow of any alternative except the highest and purest admission of a perishable and frail creature into the very sanctuary of the Divine glory ? Surely on Sinai and in the cave of Horeb such loving intercourse of almost friendship was held.

But the history of the Church soon unfolds to us a bright page, on which is emblazoned, as its title, CONTEMPLATION. At the very time when martyrs are shedding their blood and receiving the highest homage and praise, the Church, which so loves and honours them, reveres scarcely less the hundreds who fled from the very persecutions which the martyrs encountered and overcame. And the reason was, that the anchorets and cenobites, who retired to the desert and did not again return to the world after peace was restored to the Church, but swelled their numbers to thousands, were considered by her no less conquerors of the world and triumphers over the weakness of nature. Their lives of solitude and

c

silence were not idle, for they laboured with their hands for their slender sustenance; but this was expressly the rule of their lives, that even while their hands were at work, their minds should be fixed on God. And hours of the dark night had no other occupation.

It was this power of fixed and unflagging contemplation which sustained them through eighty, often, and a hundred years of seclusion. Many were men of refined minds and high education, who, in their thoughtful meditative lives, must be supposed to have attained the highest refinement of devout application to spiritual things which can be enjoyed on earth. And what pious solitaries thus gained in the desert of the Thebais, our own hermits, like Guthlake, and monks, like Cuthbert, as surely possessed. Without the peaceful enjoyment of such a sweet interior reward, their lives would have been intolerable.

So necessary does the power of communing with God alone, and ' face to face,' appear to every class of Christians, that not only the ascetics of the Eastern Church, or the mystics of the Western, profess to possess it, but even the least enthusiastic forms of religion claim, or admit it. Jacob Böhme and Swedenborg have found plenty of admirers : the latter is still leader of a sect. It would be invidious to enter into a comparison between the writings of these men and the volumes before us. We refer to them only as evidence that every form of Christianity feels the want of some transcendental piety, which bears the soul beyond the dominion and almost out of the prison of the ' body of death,' and allows it a free and familiar intercourse with God, as of spirit with spirit.

When, however, perusing the writings of St. John, the reader will find no symptom of fanaticism, no arrogation of superior privileges, of inspirations, Divine guidance, or angelic ministrations, as are to be found in pretended mystics. There is scarcely an allusion to himself, except occasionally to apologise for being so unequal to the sublime doctrines which he is unfolding, or for the rudeness of his style. Never, for a moment, does he let us know that he is communicating to us the treasures of his own experience, or describing his own sensations. One sees and knows it. A man who writes a handbook of travel need not tell us whether or no he has passed over the route himself. We feel if he has, by the minuteness of his details, by the freshness of his descriptions, by the exactness of his acquaintance with men and things.

Then, no one who had not tasted, and relished, the sweetness of the spiritual food prepared by him, could possibly treat of it with such zest ;

its delicious flavour is on the lips that speak about it. Nor need the reader imagine that he will hear from this humble and holy man accounts of visions, or ecstasies, or marvellous occurrences to himself or others ; or rules or means for attaining supernatural illuminations or miraculous gifts. No ; he proposes to guide any pupil, who feels drawn by God, to supreme love of Him, and towards those regions of contemplative prayer in which He often communicates Himself most intimately to the human soul ; but only through a dark and painful road, from which all joy and almost consolation is excluded.

It is now time to lay before the reader an outline, though imperfect, of what he will find in the volumes before him. The [two first] contain two treatises, embodying what may be called the portion of mystical instruction, most fully and excellently imparted by St. John.

It may be considered a rule in this highest spiritual life, that before it is attained there must be a period of severe probation, lasting often many years, and separating it from the previous state, which may have been one of most exalted virtue. Probably many whom the Catholic Church honours as saints have never received this singular gift. But in reading the biography of such as have been favoured with it, we shall invariably find that the possession of it has been preceded, not only by a voluntary course of mortification of sense, fervent devotion, constant meditation, and separation from the world, but also by a trying course of dryness, weariness of spirit, insipidity of devotional duties, and, what is infinitely worse, dejection, despondency, temptation to give all up in disgust, and almost despair. During this tremendous probation, the soul is dark, parched, and wayless, as ' earth without water,' as one staggering across a desert ; or, to rise to a nobler illustration, like Him, remotely, Who lay on the ground on Olivet, loathing the cup which He had longed for, beyond the sweet chalice which He had drunk with His apostles just before.

Assuming, as we do, that this trial comes upon the soul from God, its purpose is clear. That sublime condition to which it aspires, and is called, of spiritual union with infinite holiness, and of the nearest approach allowable to the closer gazing of blessed spirits into the unfathomable glory, requires a purity like gold in the crucible, and a spiritualising unclothing of whatever can be cast off, of our earthly and almost of our corporeal existence. The soul is to be winged, strongly as the eagle, gently as the dove,* to

---

* ' They shall take wings as eagles ; they shall run and not be weary ' (Isa. xl. 31). ' Who will give me wings like a dove, and I will fly and be at rest ? ' (Psalm liv. 7).

leave all this world behind it, and seek a sweet repose.

Detachment and purity are the reasons for this intermediate state of desolation; detachment not merely from outward objects and from visible bonds, but from our own wills and desires, however virtuous; detachment from our own ways of even seeking God, and still more from our sensible enjoyment of devotion, and the very sweetness of His service. There must be no trust in one's own intellect, where faith alone can guide through the deep darkness; no reliance upon the ordinary aids to contemplation, for the very impulses and first thrilling touches of love must come from God's delicate hand; no impatience for release, no desire to return back. It is an earthly purgatory, in which all dross is painfully drained out, all straw and stubble burnt up.

And what is the result? The soul has indeed been brought into a state little below that of angels; but it has given proof of a love than which theirs cannot be higher. That dark period of hard probation has completely inured her to fidelity to God, not for the sake of His rewards, not for the happiness of His service even here below, but for His own dear and good sake, because He is *her* God. And this persevering and persisting love of Him, without a ray or even a glimmering of the brightness of His countenance to light and cheer the dreary path, has surely, by gentle patience, won a returning love beyond the claims of ordinarily virtuous souls.

It is after this often long, but always severe, trial of faithful love, that what one may call the mystical espousals of God with the soul take place ; when its spiritual existence may be said to have been raised into a heavenly sphere ; when the exercise of that sublime privilege of contemplation has become so habitual, that scarce do the knees touch the ground in prayer than the affections flash upwards from the heart, and are embosomed and absorbed at once in almost blissful fruition in God's mighty love. And when the body is busy with the affairs of life, these no more hinder the familiar colloquies and the burning glances of affection directed to the one exclusive Ruler of the soul, than did the slim and light palm-leaves woven by the desert anchoret distract his thoughts.

This happy consummation of both trials and desires forms the subject of mystical treatises by many who have enjoyed it. St. John does not, except incidentally, dwell upon it. He does not systematically deal with those who bask on the summit of that spiritual Thabor ; he only guides the pilgrim to it. The ascent to the mystical mountain is rugged and steep ; the journey can

only be made in the darkness of probationary
privations of inward light and joy. Hence the
titles of his two great treatises—*The Ascent of
Mount Carmel ; The Obscure Night of the Soul.*

Each of these works may be said to go over the
same ground, though without repetitions, or
even tiresome similarities. To each is prefixed
a poem of eight stanzas, which form not merely
an introduction, but an argument rather, to a
full dissertation on mystical science. But our
author does not go beyond the two or three first
strophes in his commentary, which often expands
to many chapters : copious, most methodical
and rich upon one only line.

Mount Carmel is his natural type of the spiritual
mount ; for there, dwelt his ' Father Elias '
(*Ascent*, bk. II., ch. xx. 2), whom the Carmelites
revere as their model and founder ; and there
in a dark cavern he spake with God, and even
caught a glimpse of His glorious being, in His
might, and in His gentleness (3 Kings xix. 8).
Up, up, slowly but warily, he guides his scholar
along the steep and perilous ascent. He may be
compared to the Alpine guide who, himself
familiar with the craggy path and sure of his
steps, is all solicitude for his inexperienced charge,
and watches and directs every movement. He
makes him keep his eyes intent on the rude path
before his feet, or on the slippery stair which he

has cut out for them. He does not allow him to look down into the valley below, beautiful though it be, lest his head turn giddy, and he topple over the bluff precipice ; nor to gaze upwards, in immature hope, towards the bright pinnacles which reflect and refract the sun's rays, lest he become weary at their distance, and blinded by their brilliancy, and unable to pick his steps. Now the faithful guide takes his hand and leads him ; now he bids 'him rely on his trusty pole, throwing his weight upon it ; now he encourages him to gather all his strength, and bound over the yawning crevasse. And so in the end he lands his charge safe upon the high and dizzy summit, whence he may look around, and above, and downwards, in safety, and enjoy a sweet repose and a refreshing banquet. So careful, so minute, so tender, and so resolute is the guidance of St. John in *The Ascent of Mount Carmel*.

And through *The Obscure Night*, no less safe by its prudence and encouraging by its firmness, is his leadership to the soul. The twofold night, that of sense and that of the spirit, may be securely traversed under his direction, and the soul return to a daylight sevenfold brighter than that of the ordinary sun.

After thus attempting, however imperfectly, to give an outline of St. John's principal treatises on the spiritual life, no space remains to say anything about the beautiful writings which fill the [third and fourth] volumes. We are mistaken if many readers, who have not courage or disposition to master the abstruser and sublimer doctrines and precepts of the [two first], will not peruse with delight the more practical and cheerful maxims of the [two last], and even find exquisite satisfaction in those lessons of Divine love, and in those aphorisms of a holy life which are adapted for every devout soul.

Before closing this Preface, it is a mere act of justice to say, that the translation of these difficult works has been made with a care seldom bestowed upon such books, when rendered from a foreign language. So simple, so clear, and so thoroughly idiomatic is this version, that the reader will never have to read a sentence twice from any obscurity of language, however abstruse the subject may be. Indeed, he will almost find a difficulty in believing that the work is a translation, and has not been written originally as he reads it, in his own tongue.

LONDON,
February 23, 1864.

.*.* The first edition was in two volumes, but this is in four; hence the words placed in square brackets.

INTRODUCTION

THE fourth volume of the works of St. John of the Cross contains the last of his treatises on mystical theology, the explanation of *The Living Flame of Love,* which by many is considered the most sublime of the four ; and also some smaller writings, namely a series of Spiritual Instructions and Precautions, a collection of Letters, Maxims selected from his various works, and Poems.

The Living Flame of Love is a piece of poetry composed during or immediately after his imprisonment at Toledo. Condemned to involuntary rest and complete seclusion, deprived of every earthly comfort, even to a change of linen, during nine months, with only so much light as was indispensable for reading his breviary, and nothing but foul air to breathe, St. John lived in intimate and uninterrupted communion with God, pouring forth his soul in verses, not merely of literary merit, but replete with an exalted, rapturous love of the Spouse of his soul. In later years, when prior of Granada (1584), he was requested by his penitent, Doña Ana de Mercado y Peñalosa, widow, since 1579, of Don Juan de Guevara, to write an explanation of this canticle. He yielded to her request, says Mr. Lewis,* with great unwillingness, because the hymn is of matters so interior and spiritual as to be beyond the compass of human speech. As the *Living Flame* was composed about the same time as the *Spiritual Canticle*, the explanations of these two poems were also written about the same period ; and as the former poem is a continuation of the latter, so the commentary to that supplements the commentary to this. ' In the former stanzas,' says St. John in the Prologue, ' I spoke of the highest degree of perfection to which it is possible to attain in this life, transformation in God ; yet these, the explanation of which I now propose to undertake, speak of that love still more perfect and complete in the same state of transformation.' †

It should be understood that in this new work St. John supplies an answer to a question which must have presented itself to the reader

---

* *Life of St. John of the Cross*, by David Lewis, p. 188.
† *Infra* p 2.

of the *Spiritual Canticle*. In his first treatises the author accompanied the soul on the long and arduous journey, typically described as the *Ascent of Mount Carmel* and the *Dark Night*, which may last many years. Emerging from the terrifying darkness it finds itself in that blissful state, technically called *Espousals of the soul*, of which the *Spiritual Canticle* gives a glowing picture. Now the question arises : Can this state be permanent ? or is it just a last glorious ray before the sun sets and the eyes close in death, and the soul stands before the great white throne ? or is it a climax in the spiritual life, to be followed by a return into insignificance ? or can there be many such climaxes in the course of a single life, just as there are many snow-capped peaks in a mountain range ? We shall endeavour to answer these questions to the best of our knowledge, which, however, is strictly limited.

In the first place we must repeat what we have said in the Introduction to the *Dark Night*, namely that St. John states an extreme case ; for one soul that passes through the utter darkness of desolation, hundreds or thousands are being tried more or less sharply, but not by any

means to the same extent. Likewise, hundreds
or thousands come forth from the trial victori-
ously, while perhaps only one among so many
reaches the heights described in the *Spiritual
Canticle*. It goes almost without saying that
this is the one that has been tried most severely.
For the vast majority there may be many climaxes,
but only relative ones, as there may have been
many purgations, none of them so very searching. The reason is that but few have the
courage to undergo the active and passive purgation to the extent required by St. John. No
one respects the free will of [man more than
God does ; He forces no one to become a saint,
though He calls and allures many. Few are
generous enough to mortify every desire, every
pleasure, every gratification of sense or spirit
so completely as to absolutely empty the soul
of everything created. Now it is certain that
the subsequent exaltation is proportionate to
the antecedent humiliation. For the many, therefore, there may be many partial purgations,
succeeded by partial exaltations, while for the
few there is but one purgation, thorough in extent
and intensity, and this is followed by what St.
John calls a ' transformation ' as complete as

the previous cleansing. From what the present writer has gathered from lives of saints and biographies of saintly persons it would appear that this transformation is not as a rule postponed until the end of life, but occurs earlier. For man is created to labour in the vineyard of the Lord, and it would be strange if the Lord called away the workman just at the moment he becomes supremely fit for his work. What, then, happens to him during his subsequent career upon earth ? It would seem that the overflowing sweetness, happiness, and bliss described in the *Spiritual Canticle* are taken away, or rather absorbed, while the vigour, the merit, the aptitude for frequent transient acts of union with God remain, or rather increase. Thus, further progress is possible; not, indeed, in the sense that a further and higher state could be reached, for there remains only one more state, namely that of perpetual union, reserved for the next life ; but there may be an indefinite progress in the same state of transformation, for the soul is called to become like unto God, Who, being Himself infinite, must ever be infinitely above it, though it may go on for ever drawing nearer and nearer to Him. This last stage of the journey

forms the argument of the *Living Flame of Love*.
It would be a mistake to think that the point
reached in the *Spiritual Canticle* marks the
limit of the soul's potentialities, and that, having
reached this, nothing remains to be done but to
rest and enjoy the gain. Not only has the soul
now a wider scope for exterior work, being a
perfect instrument in the hand of a perfect
artist, but even its interior work or its co-opera-
tion with God must not cease for one moment.
There must be no relaxation in self-denial.
Though it be true that the preservation of a
habit is easier than the acquiring thereof, there
is great danger that slight neglect might lead to
the loss of habitual self-renunciation. To this
end the grace of perseverance is indispensable.
St. Paul says : ' Not as though I had already
attained, or were already perfect, but I follow
after, if I may by any means apprehend, wherein
I am also apprehended by Christ Jesus' (Phil.
iii. 12). Nor are the trials peculiar to this stage
lighter than those proper for the time of purgation, although they differ in kind. For there
they served for the purpose of penance and
mortification, while here they are a participation
in the Passion of our Lord. ' But if you partake

in the sufferings of Christ,' says St. Peter, 'rejoice that when His glory shall be revealed, you may also be glad with exceeding joy ' (1 St. Pet. iv. 13). Hence the hunger and thirst for crosses and trials and ignominy for which many saints were remarkable. St. Teresa had reached the state described in the Seventh Mansion of the *Interior Castle* (which corresponds to that pictured in the *Living Flame of Love*) in 1577; and soon afterwards she told one of her companions that she did not consider it possible to advance farther in this life in the way of prayer, nor even to wish to do so. Yet the remaining five years of life brought her trials compared with which those of her earlier years were but as child's play. St. John of the Cross is another instance. When writing the explanation of the *Living Flame of Love* he certainly recorded his own experience-Yet the keenest sufferings, particularly that of being ' despised,' especially by those to whose respect he was entitled in the highest degree, were reserved for the last years of his life. So far from striking an insensible, stoic soul, these tribulations are the lot of most refined, and therefore most sensitive, hearts, which revel in sufferings for the sake of the *sponsus sanguinum* (Exod. iv. 25).

d

In another way this last period differs also from that of the night of purgation. There the absence of heavenly visitations is an integral part of the trial. Here, there may be occasional seasons of desolation, but they alternate with prolonged periods of intimate companionship, more efficacious if less violent than during the time of spiritual exaltation. The Bridegroom may indeed hide His face, but His presence is nearly always felt. Like an ardent lover who bears the thought and remembrance of his beloved uppermost in his mind, the soul in this stage dwells continually on the thought of the Bridegroom. Such a state may continue for some years, but not for many; because this world being essentially imperfect, a soul that has reached the highest possible degree of perfection is out of place in it; and, besides, the Bridegroom will not leave it long in this exile, but hastens to unite it to Himself for evermore. What a fearful thought that there should be many who were called to fill the highest ranks of the heavenly hierarchy but who lacked the required generosity and courage in the initial stages, and forfeited thereby an everlasting crown.

St. John of the Cross wrote the treatise on

the *Living Flame of Love* twice. Neither of the originals seems to be extant, but there are copies of each version : one in the library of the Carmelite Fathers at Alba de Tormes, and the other in the National Library at Madrid (No. 6,624). A third one, of less importance, belongs to the Carmelite Fathers at Burgos ; this was copied in the eighteenth century from a manuscript belonging to the nuns of Palencia, but now lost. The second version differs greatly from the first, not in essentials but in innumerable details, showing how very carefully St. John wrote, weighing every word and every shade of expression, so as to convey his exact meaning. In this point, as in some others, he is the direct opposite of St. Teresa, who used to write incredibly fast, rarely perusing what she had written before, not even after a long interruption, and seldom revising her previous writings. Unfortunately the critical edition of the works of St. John, prepared in the eighteenth century by Fr. Andres de la Encarnación, has never been published, and students still have to rely on the unsatisfactory text of the first editors. But there is every prospect that a thoroughly reliable edition will shortly appear ; it is in the hands of competent scholars, who for several years have been collecting and collating the original manuscripts as well as the earliest and best transcripts, and who have already given proof of the thoroughness of their labours. We have been able to avail ourselves of their work in restoring a long and important passage which for some reason or other had been omitted in all former editions, Spanish as well as foreign.* The same editors announce also the recovery of many hitherto unpublished writings. Although eagerly expecting the publication of their work we did not dare to postpone the issue of this volume any longer, as many readers of the former manifested their impatience.

It is hoped that the new edition will contain valuable additions to the correspondence of the saint. The older editions contained but ten letters, the first by Mr. Lewis seventeen, the second, of which this is a reprint eighteen; but it would seem that further letters must be preserved in various places. Even so, his correspondence falls far short of that of St. Teresa; he had not the taste for sustained correspondence, and it evidently cost him much to commit his

---

* Fr. Gerardo de San Juan de la Cruz. *Un trozo inedito de la ' Llama de Amor viva,'* in the periodical *El Monte Carmelo.* Burgos, 1910, p. 801. See *infra,* pp. 16–21.

thoughts to paper ; moreover, during the troubles
in which he was involved during the greater
part of his life, his letters were destroyed by the
recipients for safety's sake. Still, we may look
forward to the results of a tardy gleaning.

The earlier editions contain a collection of a
hundred Maxims culled from his writings (now
partly lost or mislaid) and from his oral instructions. These have been augmented from his
known works, and brought to the number of
three hundred and sixty-three by Fray Antonio
Arbiol, in the work *Mystica Fundamental; or, El
Religioso Perfecto*, published at Madrid in 1761.

The Poems are reprinted from Mr. Lewis's
second edition. In the first he gave the first
three, that is, those which form the argument of
the mystical treatises, in blank verse, as they
occurred in the respective works. But in the
second he added a rhymed and rhythmical version.
The fourth poem is a glose on the words ' I live
and yet not I,' on which St. Tersea, too, wrote
two sets of verses. Since the appearance of
Mr. Lewis's second edition two more manuscripts
of verses by St. John have been discovered, one
at the National Library at Madrid (No. 6,296),
and the other in the archives of the Carmelite

nuns of Pampelona. Each contains three new poems which unmistakably bear marks of the spirit of the holy friar stamped on them.* They are published here in the elegant version prepared for this edition by the Benedictine nuns of Stanbrook.

One little treatise, entitled *The Thorns of the Spirit*, will be found in some of the Spanish editions of the works of St. John. It is also translated into French,† but not into English. The revisers of the writings of the saint left the question of its authenticity open ; the present writer is not acquainted with the external evidence for or against it, and can only form an opinion from internal criteria ; it appears to him that the style and the manner of treating the subject-matter are very unlike the acknowledged works of St. John. It might be argued that circumstances of which we have no knowledge might have induced the author to adopt a style different from that of the rest of his works ; but against this we feel bound to say that the whole spirit of the treatise is so far removed from what

* Fr. Angel-Maria de Sta Teresa. *Poesias de San Juan de la Cruz.* Burgos, 1904.
† R. P. Athanase de l'Immaculée Conception. *Traité des Epines de l'Esprit de St. Jean de la Croix.* Paris, Oudin, 1896.

we believe to have been the spirit of this great mystic that it would require very strong external evidence to make us admit the claim to authenticity. The work is divided into eight colloquies between the Spouse and the Bridegroom, and gives valuable instructions on mental prayer, frequent communion, and various scruples. It is undoubtedly the work of a Carmelite confessor, and cannot but give consolation to afflicted souls, but in our opinion it bears no trace of the master-hand of St. John of the Cross. We have therefore refrained from including it among these volumes.

BENEDICT ZIMMERMAN,
PRIOR O.C.D.

ST. LUKE'S, WINCANTON,
January 6, 1912.

P.S.—Since this Introduction was written the first volume of the critical Spanish edition, containing a preliminary essay, the Life of St. John, and the *Ascent of Mount Carmel*, has appeared under the title, *Obras del Místico Doctor San Juan de la Cruz, Edición crítica.* By Fray Gerardo de San Juan de la Cruz. Toledo, 1912.

B. Z.

THE LIVING FLAME OF LOVE

PROLOGUE

IT is not without some unwillingness that, at the requests of others, I enter upon the explanation of the four stanzas because they relate to matters so interior and spiritual as to baffle the powers of language. The spiritual transcends the sensual, and he speaks but indifferently of the mind of the spirit who has not a spiritual mind himself. I have, therefore, in consideration of my own defects, put off this matter until now. But now that our Lord seems in some way to have opened to me the way of knowledge herein, and to have given me some fervour of spirit, I have resolved to enter on the subject. I know too well that of myself I can say nothing to the purpose on any subject, how much less then on a matter of such depth and substance as this! What is mine here will be nothing but the defects and errors, and I therefore submit the whole to the better judgment and discretion of our Holy Mother the Catholic Roman Church, under whose guidance no one goeth astray. And now having said this, I will venture, in reliance on the Holy Writings, to give utterance to what I may have learned, observing at the same time, that all I say falls far short of that which passes in this intimate union of the soul with God.

2. There is nothing strange in the fact that God bestows favours so great and so wonderful upon those souls whom He is pleased to comfort. For if we consider that it is God Himself as God, and with infinite love and goodness, Who bestows them ; and this being the case, they will not seem unreasonable, for He hath said Himself that the Father and the Son and the Holy Ghost will come to him that loves Him, and will dwell in him.* And this is accomplished in making such an one live and abide in the Father, the Son, and the Holy Ghost, in the life of God, as it shall be explained in the stanzas that follow.

3. In the former stanzas I spoke of the highest degree of perfection to which it is possible to attain in this life, transformation in God ; † yet these, the explanation of which I now propose to undertake, speak of that love still more perfect and complete in the same state of transformation. For though it is true that the former and the present stanzas refer to one and the same state of transformation, and that no soul can pass beyond it as

---

* St. John xiv. 23.

† See *Spiritual Canticle*, Stanza xxvi. 4, 14 ; xxxviii. 2 ; xxxix. 20.

such, still with time and habits of devotion, the soul is more perfected and grounded in it. Thus, when a log of wood is set on fire, and when it is transformed into fire and united with it, the longer it burns and the hotter the fire, the more it glows until sparks and flames are emitted from it.

4. So too the soul—and this is the subject of these stanzas—when transformed, and glowing interiorly in the fire of love, is not only united with the divine fire, but becomes a living flame, and itself conscious of it. The soul speaks of this with an intimate delicious sweetness of love, burning in its own flame, dwelling upon the various marvellous effects wrought within it. These effects I now proceed to describe, following the same method : that is, I shall first transcribe the four stanzas, then each separately, and finally each line by itself as I explain them.

STANZAS *

I

O Living Flame of Love,
That woundest tenderly
My soul in its inmost depth !
As thou art no longer grievous,
Perfect thy work, if it be thy will,
Break the web of this sweet encounter.

* These stanzas were written after the saint's escape from the prison of the friars in Toledo, and the commentary on them was written at the request of doña Ana de Peñalosa, one of his penitents.

II

O sweet burn !
O delicious wound !
O tender hand ! O gentle touch !
Savouring of everlasting life,
And paying the whole debt,
By slaying Thou hast changed death into life.

III

O lamps of fire,
In the splendours of which
The deep caverns of sense,
Dim and dark,
With unwonted brightness
Give light and warmth together to their Beloved !

IV

How gently and how lovingly
Thou wakest in my bosom,
Where alone Thou secretly dwellest ;
And in Thy sweet breathing
Full of grace and glory,
How tenderly Thou fillest me with Thy love.

EXPLANATION OF THE FIRST STANZA

THE bride of Christ, now feeling herself to be all on fire
in the divine union, and that rivers of living waters are
flowing from her belly, as Christ our Lord said * they
would flow from the like souls, believes that, as she is

* St. John vii. 38.

transformed in God with such vehemence and so intimately possessed by Him, so richly adorned with gifts
and graces, she is near unto bliss, and that a slender veil
only separates her from it. Seeing, too, that this sweet
flame of love burning within her, each time it touches her,
makes her as it were glorious with foretaste of glory, so
much so that whenever it absorbs and assails her, it seems
to be admitting her to everlasting life, and to rend the
veil of her mortality, she addresses herself, with a great
longing, to the flame, which is the Holy Ghost, and prays
Him to destroy her mortal life in this sweet encounter,
and bestow upon her in reality what He seems about to
give, namely, perfect glory, crying : ' O living flame of
love.'

' O living flame of love.'

2. In order to express the fervour and reverence with
which the soul is speaking in these four stanzas, it begins
them with ' O ' and ' How,' which are significant of
great earnestness, and whenever uttered show that something passes within that is deeper than the tongue can
tell. ' O ' is the cry of strong desire, and of earnest sup-
plication, in the way of persuasion. The soul employs
it in both senses here, for it magnifies and intimates its
great desire, calling upon love to end its mortal life.

3. This flame of love is the Spirit of the Bridegroom,
the Holy Ghost, of whose presence within itself the soul

is conscious, not only as fire which consumes it, and transforms it in sweet love, but as a fire burning within it, sending forth a flame which bathes it in glory and recreates it with the refreshment of everlasting life. The work of the Holy Ghost in a soul transformed in His love is this : His interior action within it is to kindle it and set it on fire ; this is the burning of love, in union with which the will loves most deeply, being now one by love with that flame of fire. And thus the soul's acts of love are most precious, and even one of them more meritorious than many elicited not in the state of transformation. The transformation in love differs from the flame of love as a habit differs from an act, or as the glowing fuel from the flames it emits, the flames being the effect of the fire which is there burning.

4. Hence then we may say of the soul which is transformed in love, that its ordinary state is that of the fuel in the midst of the fire ; that the acts of such a soul are the flames which rise up out of the fire of love, vehement in proportion to the intensity of the fire of union, and to the rapture and absorption of the will in the flame of the Holy Ghost ; rising like the angel who ascended to God in the flame which consumed the holocaust of Manue.* And as the soul, in its present condition, cannot elicit these acts without a special inspiration of the

* Judg. xiii. 20.

Holy Ghost, all these acts must be divine, in so far as the soul is under the special influence of God. Hence then it seems to the soul, as often as the flame breaks forth, causing it to love sweetly with a heavenly disposition, that its life everlasting is begun, and that its acts are divine in God.

5. This is the language in which God addresses purified and stainless souls, namely, words of fire. ' Thy word,' saith the Psalmist, ' is a vehement fire.' * And in Jeremias we read, ' are not My words as a fire ? saith our Lord.' † His ' words,' we learn from Himself, ' are spirit and life ; ' ‡ the power and efficacy of which are felt by such souls as have ears to hear ; pure souls full of love. But those souls whose palate is not healthy, whose desire is after other things cannot perceive the spirit and life of His words. And therefore the more wonderful the words of the Son of God, the more insipid they are to some who hear them, because of the impurity in which they live.

6. Thus, when He announced the doctrine of the Holy Eucharist, a doctrine full of sweetness and of love, ' many of His disciples went back.' § If such persons as these have no taste for the words of God which He speaks inwardly to them, it is not to be supposed that all others

---

* Ps. cxviii. 140.　　　　† Jerem. xxiii. 29.
‡ St. John vi. 64.　　　　§ *Ib.* vi. 67.

are like them. St. Peter loved the words of Christ, for
he replied, ' Lord, to whom shall we go ?   Thou hast the
words of eternal life.' *   The woman of Samaria forgot
the water, and ' left her waterpot ' † at the well, because
of the sweetness of the words of God.

7.   And now when the soul has drawn so near unto
God as to be transformed in the flame of love, when the
Father and the Son and the Holy Ghost are in com-
munion with it, is it anything incredible to say that it
has a foretaste—though not perfectly, because this life
admits not of it—of everlasting life in this fire of the Holy
Ghost ?   This is the reason why this flame is said to be a
living flame, not because it is not always living, but
because its effect is to make the soul live spiritually in
God, and to be conscious of such a life, as it is written,
' My heart and my flesh have rejoiced toward the living
God.' ‡   The Psalmist makes use of the word ' living,'
not because it was necessary, for God is ever-living, but
to show that the body and the spirit had a lively feeling
of God ; that is the rejoicing in the living God.   Thus, in
this flame, the soul has so vivid a sense of God, and a
perception of Him so sweet and delicious, that it cries
out : ' O living flame of love ! '

> ' That woundest tenderly.'

8.   That is, Thou touchest me tenderly in Thy love.

---

* St. John. vi. 69. † *Ib.* iv. 28. ‡ Ps. lxxxiii. 3.

For when this flame of divine life wounds the soul with
the gentle languishing for the life of God, it wounds it
with so much endearing tenderness, and softens it so that
it melts away in love. The words of the bride in the
Canticle are now fulfilled in the soul. ' My soul melted
when He spoke.' * This is the effect in the soul when
God speaks.

9. But how can we say that it wounds the soul, when
there is nothing to wound, seeing that it is all consumed
in the fire of love ? It is certainly marvellous ; for as fire
is never idle, but in continual movement, flashing in one
direction, then in another, so love, the function of which
is to wound, so as to cause love and joy, when it exists in
the soul as a living flame, darts forth its most tender
flames of love, causing wounds, exerting joyously all the
arts and wiles of love as in the palace of its wedding
feast. So Assuerus exhibited his riches, and the glory of
his power at ' the wedding and marriage of Esther ; ' †
and so is wrought in the soul what is read in the Proverbs :
I ' was delighted every day . . . playing in the world,
and My delights were to be with the children of men,' ‡
that is to give Myself to them. This wounding, therefore,
which is the ' playing ' of divine wisdom, is the flames of
those tender touches which touch the soul continually,
touches of the fire of love which is never idle. And of

* Cant, v. 6.   † Esth. ii. 18.   ‡ Prov. viii. 30, 31.

these flashings of the fire it is said that they wound the soul in its inmost substance.

' My soul in its inmost depth.'

10. The feast of the Holy Ghost is celebrated in the substance of the soul, which is inaccessible to the devil, the world, and the flesh ; and therefore the more interior the feast, the more secure, substantial, and delicious is it. For the more interior it is, the purer it is ; and the greater the purity, the greater the abundance, frequency, and universality of God's communication of Himself ; and thus the joy of the soul and spirit is so much the greater, for it is God Himself Who is the author of all this, and the soul doeth nothing of itself, in the sense I shall immediately explain.

11. And inasmuch as the soul cannot work naturally here, nor make any efforts of its own otherwise than through the bodily senses and by their help—of which it is in this case completely free, and from which it is most detached—the work of the soul is solely to receive what God communicates, Who alone in the depths of the soul, without the help of the senses, can influence and direct it, and operate within it. Thus, then, all the movements of such a soul are divine, and though of God, still they are the soul's, because God effects them within it, itself willing them and assenting to them.

12. The expression, ' inmost depth,' implies other

depths of the soul less profound, and it is necessary to consider this. In the first place the soul, regarded as spirit, has neither height nor depth of greater or less degree in its own nature, as bodies have which have bulk. The soul has no parts, neither is there any difference between its interior and exterior, for it is uniform ; it has no depths of greater or less profundity, nor can one part of it be more enlightened than another, as is the case with physical bodies, for the whole of it is enlightened uniformly at once.

13. Setting aside this signification of depth, material and measureable, we say that the inmost depth of the soul is there where its being, power, and the force of its action and movement penetrate and cannot go further. Thus fire, or a stone, tend by their natural force to the centre of their sphere, and cannot go beyond it, or help resting there, unless some obstacle intervene. Accordingly, when a stone lies on the ground it is said to be within its centre, because within the sphere of its active motion, which is the element of earth, but not in the inmost depth of that centre, the middle of the earth, because it has still power and force to descend thither, provided all that hinders it be taken away. So when it shall have reached the centre of the earth, and is incapable of further motion of its own, we say of it that it is then in its inmost or deepest centre.

14. The centre of the soul is God. When the soul

shall have reached Him, according to its essence, and according to the power of its operations, it will then have attained to its ultimate and deepest centre in God. This will be when the soul shall love Him, comprehend Him, and enjoy Him with all its strength. When, however, the soul has not attained to this state, though it be in God, Who is the centre of it by grace and communion with Him, still if it can move further and is not satisfied, though in the centre, it is not in the deepest centre, because there is still room for it to advance.

15. Love unites the soul with God, and the greater its love the deeper does it enter into God, and the more is it centered in Him. According to this way of speaking we may say, that as the degrees of love, so are the centres which the soul finds in God. These are the many mansions of the Father's house.* Thus, a soul which has but one degree of love is already in God, Who is its centre : for one degree of love is sufficient for our abiding in Him in the state of grace. If we have two degrees of love we shall then have found another centre, more interiorly in God ; and if we have three we shall have reached another and more interior centre still.

16. But if the soul shall have attained to the highest degree of love, the love of God will then wound it in its inmost depth or centre ; and the soul will be transformed

* St. John xiv. 2.

and enlightened in the highest degree in its substance, faculties, and strength, until it shall become most like unto God. The soul in this state may be compared to crystal, lucid and pure ; the greater the light thrown upon it, the more luminous it becomes by the concentration thereof, until at last it seems to be all light and undistinguishable from it ; it being then so illumined, and to the utmost extent, that it seems to be one with the light itself.

17. The flame wounds the soul in its inmost depth ; that is, it wounds it when it touches the very depths of its substance, power and force. This expression implies that abundance of joy and bliss, which is the greater and the more tender, the more vehemently and substantially the soul is transformed and centred in God. It greatly surpasses that which occurs in the ordinary union of love, for it is in proportion to the greater heat of the fire of love which now emits the living flame. The soul which has the fruition only of the ordinary union of love may be compared, in a certain sense, to the ' fire ' of God which is in Sion, that is in the Church Militant ; while the soul which has the fruition of glory so sweet may be compared to ' His furnace in Jerusalem,' * which means the vision of peace.

18. The soul in the burning furnace is in a more peace-

* Is. xxxi. 9.

ful, glorious, and tender union, the more the flame of the furnace transcends the fire of ordinary love. Thus the soul, feeling that the living flame ministers to it all good—divine love brings all blessings with it—cries out : ' O living flame of love, that woundest tenderly.' The cry of the soul is : O kindling burning love, how tenderly dost thou make me glorious by thy loving movements in my greatest power and strength, giving me a divine intelligence according to the capacity of my understanding, and communicating love according to the utmost freedom of my will ; that is, thou hast elevated to the greatest height, by the divine intelligence, the powers of my understanding in the most intense fervour and substantial union of my will. This ineffable effect then takes place when this flame of fire rushes upwards in the soul. The divine wisdom absorbs the soul—which is now purified and most clean—profoundly and sublimely in itself ; for ' wisdom reacheth everywhere by reason of her purity.' * It is in this absorption of wisdom that the Holy Ghost effects those glorious quiverings of His flame of which I am speaking. And as the flame is so sweet, the soul says : ' As Thou art no longer grievous.'

' As Thou art no longer grievous.'

19. Thou dost not afflict, nor vex, nor weary me as before. This flame, when the soul was in the state of

* Wisd. vii. 24.

spiritual purgation, that is, when it was entering that of contemplation, was not so friendly and sweet as it is now in the state of union. In order to explain this we must dwell a little on this point. For before the divine fire enters into the soul and unites itself to it in its inmost depth by the complete and perfect purgation and purity thereof, the flame, which is the Holy Ghost, wounds it, destroys and consumes the imperfections of its evil habits. This is the work of the Holy Ghost, Who thereby disposes the soul for its divine union and a substantial transformation in God by love. For the flame which afterwards unites itself to the soul, glorifying it, is the very same which before assailed and purified it ; just as the fire which ultimately penetrates the substance of the fuel is the very same which in the beginning darted its flames around it, playing about it, and depriving it of its ugliness until it prepared it with its heat for its own entrance into it, and transformation of it into itself.

20. The soul suffers greatly in this spiritual exercise, and endures grievous afflictions of spirit which occasionally overflow into the senses ; for then the flame is felt to be grievous, for in this state of purgation the flame does not burn brightly but is darksome, and if it gives forth any light at all it is only to show to the soul and make it feel all its miseries and defects ; neither is it sweet but painful, and if it kindles a fire of love that fire causes

torments and uneasiness ; it does not bring delight but
aridity, for although God in His kindness may send the
soul some comfort to strengthen and animate it He makes
it pay, both before and after, with sufferings and trials.
It is not a refreshing and peaceful fire, but a consuming
and searching one that makes the soul faint away and
grieve at the sight of Self ; not a glorious brightness, for
it embitters the soul and makes it miserable, owing to
the spiritual light it throws on Self, for, as Jeremias says,
God ' hath sent fire into my bones ' * or, in the words
of David ' Thou hast tried me by fire.' † Thus, at this
juncture, the soul suffers in the understanding from deep
darkness, in the will from aridity and conflict, and in
the memory from the consciousness of its miseries—for
the eye of the spiritual understanding is clear—and in
its very substance the soul suffers from poverty and dere-
liction. Dry and cold, yea, at times, even hot, nothing
gives it relief, nor has it a single good thought to con-
sole it and to help it to lift up the heart to God, for this
flame has made it ' grievous,' even as Job said when
he found himself in this plight : ' Thou art changed to
be cruel toward me.' ‡ Suffering all these things together the soul undergoes, as it were, its Purgatory, for
all happiness being taken away the torture is hardly
inferior to the torments of Purgatory.

* Lament. i. 13. † Ps. xvi. 3. ‡ Job xxx. 21.

I should scarcely know how to describe this ' grievousness,' and what the soul feels and bears in it were it not for these telling words of Jeremias : ' I am the man that see my poverty by the rod of His indignation ; He hath led me, and brought me into darkness and not into light. Only against me He hath turned, and turned again His hand all the day. My skin and my flesh He hath made old, He hath broken my bones. He hath built round about me, and He hath encompassed me with gall and labour. He hath set me in dark places, as those that are dead for ever. He hath built against me round about, that I may not get out : He hath made my fetters heavy.' * Jeremias says a great deal more besides this in the same place ; for this is the remedy and medicine chosen by God to restore health to the soul after its many infirmities, the cure being of a necessity commensurate to the disease. Here, then, the heart is ' laid upon coals to drive away all kind of devils ; ' † here, too, all its maladies are brought to light, and openly exhibited before the eyes, and thus they are cured. Whatever may have been hidden within its depths now becomes visible and palpable to the soul by the glare and heat of that fire, for previously nothing could be seen. When the flame acts upon a log of wood steam and smoke are seen to issue in evidence of humidity and frigidity which were un-

---

* Lament. iii. 1-7.   † Tobias vi. 8.

suspected beforehand. Thus the soul, near this flame, sees and feels clearly its miseries, because, O wonder ! there arise within it contraries at variance with each other, yet seated side by side, making war against each other on the battlefield of the soul, and striving, as the philosophers say, to expel each other so as to reign uppermost in the soul. The virtues and properties of God, being in the highest degree perfect, arise and make war within the soul, on the habits and properties of man which are in the highest degree imperfect. For since this flame gives forth a dazzling light it penetrates the darkness of the soul which, in its way, is profound in the extreme ; the soul now feels its natural darkness oppose the supernatural light, without feeling the supernatural light itself, for ' the darkness does not comprehend it.' * Rather, it feels its natural darkness only in so far as it is penetrated by light, for no soul can see its own darkness except by the side of the Divine light until, the darkness being dissipated, itself becomes illumined and sees the light, the eye being now made clear and strong. For an intense light is to a weak sight, or an eye that is not wholly clear, nothing but darkness, because the excess of light destroys the power of seeing. For this reason the flame was ' grievous ' to the eye of the understanding, for, being at once loving and tender, it lovingly

* St. John i. 5.

and tenderly penetrates the will which, by its nature, is arid and hard. And as hardness is discovered when contrasted with tenderness, and aridity when compared with love, so the will comes to a knowledge of its own hardness and aridity when contrasted with God, though it does not feel the love and tenderness of the flame, for hardness and aridity cannot comprehend their contraries, until, being expelled by these, the love and tenderness of God reign supreme in the will, for two contraries cannot co-exist in one subject. Similarly, the soul perceives its own smallness in comparison with the immensity of the flame, and suffers great uneasiness until the flame, acting on it, dilates it. Thus, the latter has proved ' grievous ' to the will also, for the sweet nourishment of love is insipid to a palate not yet weaned from other affections. Finally, the soul, which of itself is exceedingly poor, having nothing whatever, nor the means of procuring any satisfaction, gains a knowledge of its poverty, misery and malice by contrasting them with the riches, goodness and delights possessed by this flame, for malice does not comprehend goodness, nor poverty riches, etc., until the flame succeeds in purifying the soul, and, while transforming it, enriches, glorifies, and delights it too. In this manner the flame was at first ' grievous ' to the soul, which suffers severely in its substance and powers from the uneasiness and anguish caused by the war of contraries within its

ailing frame.   Here, God Who is all perfection, there the
habits of imperfection of the soul ; cauterising it with a
Divine fire He extirpates them and leaves a well-prepared
soil upon which He may enter with His gentle, peaceful
and glorious love, as does a flame when it gets hold of
wood.

So powerful a purgation is the lot of but few souls,
namely of those whom He intends to lift by contemplation
to some degree of union ; the more sublime that degree,
the fiercer the purification.   When He resolves to snatch
a soul from the common way of natural operations and
to lead it to the spiritual life, from meditation to contemplation—which is heavenly rather than earthly life
—and to communicate Himself by the union of love,
He begins by making Himself known to the spirit, as yet
impure and imperfect and full of evil habits.   Each one
suffers in proportion to his imperfections.   This purgation is sometimes as fierce in its way as that of Purgatory,
for the one is meant to dispose the soul for a perfect union
even here below, while the other is to enable it to see God
hereafter.   I shall say nothing here of the intention of
this cleansing, the degrees of its intensity, its operation
in the will, the understanding and the memory, in the
substance of the soul, in all its powers, or in the sensitive
part alone, nor how it may be ascertained whether it is
this or that, at what time or at which precise point of the

spiritual journey it begins, as all this has nothing to do with my present purpose ; moreover, I have fully discussed it in my treatise on the Dark Night in the Ascent of Mount Carmel.* It is enough for us to know that God, Who seeks to enter the soul by union and transformation of love, is He who previously assailed the soul, purifying it with the light and heat of His divine flame, just as it is the same fire that first disposes the wood for combustion and afterwards consumes it. Thus, the same which now is sweet, being seated within the soul, was at first ' grievous ' while assailing it from without.

21. The meaning of the whole is as follows : Thou art now not only not darkness as before, but the divine light of my understanding wherewith I behold Thee : not only dost Thou abstain from causing me to faint in my weakness, but Thou art become the strength of my will, wherein I can love and enjoy Thee, being wholly transformed by divine love. Thou art no longer grief and affliction, but rather my glory, my delight, and my liberty, seeing that the words of the Canticle may be said of me, ' Who is this that cometh up from the desert flowing with delights

---

* *Dark Night of the Soul* : Book II. The former editions, and all the translations, say ' in the treatise of the Dark Night *and* in that of the Ascent of Mount Carmel,' as if the Saint had spoken on this subject in both works. The manuscripts make the matter clear, for St. John considered the Dark Night as part of the Ascent.

leaning upon her Beloved,' * scattering love on this side and on that ?   ' Perfect Thy work, if it be Thy will.'

' Perfect Thy work, if it be Thy will.'

22.   That is, do Thou perfect the spiritual marriage in the beatific vision.   Though it is true that the soul is the more resigned the more it is transformed, when it has attained to a state so high as this, for it knows nothing and seeks nothing with a view to itself,† but only in and for the Beloved—for Charity seeks nothing but the good and glory of the Beloved—still because it lives in hope, and hope implies a want, it groans deeply—though sweetly and joyfully—because it has not fully attained to the perfect adoption of the sons of God, in which, being perfected in glory, all its desires will be satisfied.   However intimate the soul's union may be with God, it will never be satisfied here below till His 'glory shall appear; ' ‡ especially because it has already tasted, by anticipation, of its sweetness.

23.   That sweetness is such that if God had not had pity on its natural frailty and covered it with His right hand, as He did Moses, that he might not die when he saw the glory of God—for the natural powers of the soul receive comfort and delight from that right hand, rather than hurt—it would have died at each vibration of the flame, seeing that the inferior part thereof is incapable of

* Cant. viii. 5.   † 1 Cor. xiii. 5.   ‡ Ps. xvi. 15.

enduring so great and so sharp a fire. This desire of the
soul is therefore no longer painful, for its condition is now
such that all pain is over, and its prayers are offered for
the object it desires in great sweetness, joy and resignation. This is the reason why it says, ' if it be Thy will,'
for the will and desire are now so united in God, each in
its own way, that the soul regards it as its glory that the
will of God should be done in it. Such are now the
glimpses of glory, and such the love which now shines
forth, that it would argue but little love on its part if it did
not pray to be admitted to the perfect consummation of
love.

24. Moreover, the soul in the power of this sweet
communication, sees that the Holy Ghost incites it, and
invites it in most wonderful ways, and by sweet affections,
to this immeasurable glory, which He there sets before
it, saying, ' Arise, make haste, my love, my dove, my
beautiful one, and come. For winter is now past, the
rain is gone and departed. The flowers have appeared in
our land . . . . The fig-tree hath brought forth her green
figs, the flourishing vineyards have given their savour.
Arise, my love, my beautiful one, and come ; my dove
in the holes of the rock, in the hollow places of the wall,
show me thy face, let thy voice sound in mine ears, for
thy voice is sweet, and thy face comely.' *   The soul

* Cant. ii. 10–14.

hears all this spoken by the Holy Ghost in this sweet and tender flame, and therefore answers Him, saying, ' Perfect Thy work, if it be Thy will,' thereby making the two petitions which our Lord commands, ' Thy kingdom come, Thy will be done ; ' * that is, give me Thy kingdom according to Thy will, and that it may be so ' Break the web of this sweet encounter.'

' Break the web of this sweet encounter.'

25. That is, the hindrance to this so grand an affair. It is an easy thing to draw near unto God when all hindrances are set aside, and when the web that divides us from Him is broken. There are three webs to be broken before we can have the perfect fruition of God : 1. The temporal web, which comprises all created things. 2. The natural web, which comprises all mere natural actions and inclinations. 3. The web of sense, which is merely the union of soul and body ; that is, the sensitive and animal life, of which St. Paul speaks, saying, ' For we know if our earthly house of this habitation be dissolved, that we have a building of God, a house not made with hands, eternal in heaven.' †

26. The first and second web must of necessity have been broken in order to enter into the fruition of God in the union of love, when we denied ourselves in worldly things and renounced them, when our affections and

* St. Matth. vi. 10. † 2 Cor. v. 1.

desires were mortified, and when all our operations became divine. These webs were broken in the assaults of this flame when it was still grievous. In the spiritual purgation the soul breaks the two webs I am speaking of, and becomes united with God ; the third alone, the web of the life of sense remains now to be broken. This is the reason why but one web is mentioned here. For now one web alone remains, and this the flame assails not painfully and grievously as it assailed the others, but with great sweetness and delight.

27. Thus the death of such souls is most full of sweetness, beyond that of their whole spiritual life, for they die of the sweet violence of love, like the swan which sings more sweetly when death is nigh.

28. This is why the Psalmist said, ' Precious in the sight of our Lord is the death of His saints,' * for then the rivers of the soul's love flow into the sea of love, so wide and deep as to seem a sea themselves ; the beginning and the end unite together to accompany the just departing for His kingdom. ' From the ends of the earth,' in the words of Isaias, are ' heard praises, the glory of the just one,'† and the soul feels itself in the midst of these glorious encounters on the point of departing in all abundance for the perfect fruition of the kingdom, for it beholds itself pure and rich, and prepared, so far as

* Ps. cxv. 15.   † Is. xxiv. 16.

it is possible, consistently with the faith and the conditions of this life. God now permits it to behold its own beauty, and intrusts it with the gifts and graces He has endowed it with, for all this turns into love and praise without the stain of presumption or of vanity, because no leaven of imperfection remains to corrupt it.

29. When the soul sees that nothing is wanting but the breaking of the frail web of its natural life, by which its liberty is enthralled, it prays that it may be broken ; for it longs ' to be dissolved and to be with Christ,'* to burst the bonds which bind the spirit and the flesh together, that both may resume their proper state, for they are by nature different, the flesh to ' return to its earth, and the spirit unto God Who gave it.' † The mortal body, as St. John saith, ' profiteth nothing,' ‡ but is rather a hindrance to the good of the spirit. The soul, therefore, prays for the dissolution of the body, for it is sad that a life so mean should be a hindrance in the way of a life so noble.

30. This life is called a web for three reasons : 1. Because of the connection between the spirit and the flesh. 2. Because it separates the soul and God. 3. Because a web is not so thick but that light penetrates it. The connection between soul and body, in this state of per-

* Phil. i. 23.   † Eccles. xii. 7.   ‡ St. John vi. 64.

fection, is so slight a web that the divinity shines through it, now that the soul is so spiritualised, subtilised, and refined. When the power of the life to come is felt in the soul, the weakness of this life becomes manifest. Its present life seems to be but a slender web, even a spider's web, in the words of David, ' our years shall be considered as a spider,'* and even less than that, when the soul is raised to a state so high, for being raised so high, it perceives things as God does, in Whose sight.' a thousand years are as yesterday which is past,' † and before Whom ' all nations are as if they had no being at all.' ‡ In the same way all things appear to the soul as nothing, yea, itself is nothing in its own eyes, and God alone is its all.

31. It may be asked here why the soul prays for the breaking of the web rather than for its cutting or its removal, since the effect would be the same in either case. There are four reasons which determine it : 1. The expression it employs is the most proper, because it is more natural that a thing should be broken in an encounter, than that it should be cut or taken away. 2. Because love likes force, with violent and impetuous contacts, and these result in breaking rather than in cutting or taking away. 3. Because its love is so strong, it desires that the act of breaking the web may be done in a moment;

---

* Ps. lxxxix. 9.   † *Ib.* lxxxix. 4.   ‡ Is. xl. 17.

the more rapid and spiritual the act, the greater its force
and worth.

32.   The power of love is now more concentrated and
more vigorous, and the perfection of transforming love
enters the soul, as form into matter, in an instant.   Until
now there was no act of perfect transformation, only the
disposition towards it in desires and affections successively
repeated, which in very few souls attain to the perfect act
of transformation.   Hence a soul that is disposed may
elicit many more, and more intense acts in a brief period
than another soul not so disposed in a long time, for this
soul spends all its energies in the preparation of itself, and
even afterwards the fire does not wholly penetrate the fuel
it has to burn.   But when the soul is already prepared,
love enters in continuously, and the spark at the first
contact seizes on the fuel that is dry.   And thus the
enamoured soul prefers the abrupt breaking of the web
to its tedious cutting or waiting for its removal.

33.   4. The fourth reason why the soul prays for the
breaking of the web of life is its desire that it may be done
quickly : for when we cut or remove anything we do it
deliberately, when the matter is ripe, and then time and
thought become necessary ; but a violent rupture requires
nothing of the kind.   The soul's desire is not to wait for
the natural termination of its mortal life, because the
violence of its love and the disposition it is in incline it with

resignation towards the violent rupture of its natural life in the supernatural assaults of love. Moreover, it knows well that it is the way of God to call such souls to Himself before the time, that He fills them with good, and delivers them from evil, perfecting them in a short space, and bestowing upon them, through love, what they could have gained only by length of time. ' Pleasing God, he is made beloved, and living among sinners he was translated. He was taken away lest malice should change his understanding, or lest any guile deceive his soul. Being consummate in a short space, he fulfilled much time, for his soul pleased God ; for this cause He hastened to bring him out of the midst of iniquities.' * The constant practice of love is therefore a matter of the last importance, for when the soul is perfect therein, its detention here below cannot be long before it is admitted to see God face to face.

34. But why is this interior assault of the Holy Ghost called an encounter ? Though the soul is very desirous to see the end of its natural life, yet because the time is not yet come, that cannot be, and so God, to make it perfect and to raise it above the flesh more and more, assails it divinely and gloriously, and these assaults are really encounters wherein God penetrates the soul, deifies the very substance of it, and renders it as it were divine. The substance of God absorbs the soul, because He

* Wisd. iv. 10–14.

assails and pierces it to the quick by the Holy Ghost, whose communications are vehement when they are of fire as at present.   The soul says this encounter is sweet, because it has therein a lively taste of God ; not that many other touches and encounters of God, of which the soul is now the object, cease to be sweet and delicious, but on account of the supereminent sweetness of this ; for God effects it in order to detach it perfectly and make it glorious.   Hence the soul relying on His protection becomes bold, and says, ' Break the web of this sweet encounter.'

35.   The whole stanza may be paraphrased as follows : O flame of the Holy Ghost, penetrating so profoundly and so tenderly the very substance of my soul, and burning it with Thy heat, since Thou art now so gentle as to manifest Thy desire of giving Thyself wholly to me in everlasting life ; if formerly my petitions did not reach Thine ears, when I was weary and worn with love, suffering through the weakness of sense and spirit, because of my great infirmities, impurity, and little love, I prayed to be set free—for with desire hath my soul desired Thee —when my impatient love would not suffer me to submit to the conditions of this life according to Thy will—for it was Thy will that I should live—and when the previous impulses of my love were insufficient in Thy sight, because there was no substance in them ; now that I am

grown strong in love, that body and soul together do not only follow after Thee, but that my heart and my flesh rejoice in the living God * with one consent, so that I am praying for that which Thou willest I should pray for, and what Thou willest not, that I pray not for—it seems even that I could not do it, neither does it enter into my mind to do so—and as my prayers are now more efficacious and more reasonable in Thy sight, for they proceed from Thee, and Thou willest I should so pray, and as I pray in the joy and sweetness of the Holy Ghost, and ' my judgment cometh forth from Thy countenance,'† when Thou art pleased with my prayer and hearkenest to it—break Thou the slender web of this life that I may be enabled to love Thee hereafter with that fulness and abundance which my soul desires, without end for evermore.

STANZA II

O sweet burn !
O delicious wound !
O tender hand ! O gentle touch !
Savouring of everlasting life,
And paying the whole debt,
In destroying death Thou hast changed it into life.

---

* Ps. lxxxiii. 3.   † *Ib.* xvi. 2.

EXPLANATION

WE learn here that it is the Three Persons of the Most
Holy Trinity, Father, Son, and Holy Ghost, Who accomplish the divine work of union in the soul. The
'hand,' the 'touch,' and the 'burn' are in substance one
and the same ; and the three terms are employed because
they express effects peculiar to each. The 'burn' is the
Holy Ghost ; the 'hand' is the Father ; and the 'touch'
is the Son. Thus the soul magnifies the Father, the
Son, and the Holy Ghost, extolling those three grand
gifts and graces which They perfect within it, in that
They have changed death into life, transforming it in
Themselves.

2. The first of these gifts is the delicious wound,
attributed to the Holy Ghost, and so the soul calls it
the 'burn.' The second is the 'taste of everlasting life,'
attributed to the Son, and the soul calls it the 'gentle
touch.' The third is that 'gift' which is the perfect
recompense of the soul, attributed to the Father, and is
therefore called the 'tender hand.' Though the Three
Persons of the Most Holy Trinity are referred to sever-
ally, because of the operations peculiar to Each, the
soul is addressing itself to but One Essence, saying,
'Thou hast changed it into life,' for the Three Divine

Persons work together, and the whole is attributed to Each, and to All.

'O sweet burn.'

3. In the book of Deuteronomium, Moses saith, 'Our Lord God is a consuming fire,' * that is, a fire of love. And as His power is infinite, He consumes infinitely, burning with great vehemence, and transforming into Himself all He touches. But He burns everything according to the measure of its preparation, some more, others less; and also according to His own good pleasure, as, and when, and how, He will. And as this is an infinite fire of love, so when He touches the soul somewhat sharply, the burning heat within it becomes so extreme as to surpass all the fires of the world. This is the reason why this touch of God is said to be a 'burn:' for the fire there is more intense, and more concentrated, and the effect of it surpasses that of all other fires.

4. When the divine fire shall have transformed the soul into itself, the soul not only feels the burn, but itself is become wholly and entirely burnt up in this vehement fire. O how wonderful the fire of God! though so vehement and so consuming, though it can destroy a thousand worlds with more ease than the material fire can destroy a single straw, it consumes not the spirit wherein it burns, but rather, in proportion to its strength

* Deut. iv. 24.

3

and heat, delights and deifies it, burning sweetly within according to the strength which God has given. Thus, on the day of Pentecost the fire descended with great vehemence upon the Apostles, who, according to St. Gregory,* sweetly burned interiorly. The Church also says, when celebrating that event : ' The divine fire came down, not consuming but enlightening.' † For as the object of these communications is to elevate the soul, the burning of the fire does not distress it but gladdens it, does not weary it but delights it, and renders it glorious and rich. This is the reason why it is said to be sweet.

5. Thus then the blessed soul, which by the mercy of God has been burnt, knoweth all things, tasteth all things, ' whatsoever it shall do shall prosper,' ‡ against it nothing shall prevail, nothing shall touch it. It is of that soul that the Apostle said : ' The spiritual man judgeth all things, and he himself is judged of no man,'§ for ' the Spirit searcheth all things, yea, the deep things of God,' ‖ because it belongs to love to search into all that the Beloved has.

* Hom. 30 in Evangel (Whit Sunday). ' Intus facta sunt corda flammantia, quia dum Deum in ignis visione susceperunt, per amorem suaviter arserunt.'

† Brev. Rom. fer. 2 Pent. Resp .II. ad Mat. ' Advenit ignis divinus, non comburens, sed illuminans.'

‡ Ps. i. 3.   § 1 Cor. ii. 15.   ‖ *Ib.* 10.

6. O, the great glory of the souls who are worthy of this supreme fire which, having infinite power to consume and annihilate you, consumes you not, but makes you infinitely perfect in glory! Wonder not that God should elevate some souls to so high a degree, for He alone is wonderful in His marvellous works. As this burn then is so sweet—as it is here said to be—how happy must that soul be which this fire has touched! The soul would speak of it, but cannot, so it says only, ' O delicious wound.'

' O delicious wound.'

7. He Who inflicts the wound relieves, and heals while He inflicts it. It bears some resemblance to the caustic usage of natural fire, which when applied to a wound increases it, and renders a wound, which iron or other instruments occasioned, a wound of fire. The longer the caustic is applied, the more grievous the wound, until the whole matter be destroyed. Thus the divine burn of love heals the wound which love has caused, and by each application renders it greater. The healing which love brings is to wound again what was wounded before, until the soul melts away in the fire of love. So when the soul shall become wholly one wound of love it will then be transformed in love, wounded with love. For herein he who is most wounded is the most healthy, and he who is all wound is all health.

8. And yet even if the whole soul be one wound, and consequently sound, the divine burning is not intermitted ; it continues its work, which is to wound the soul with love. But then, too, its work is to soothe the healed wound, and the soul therefore cries out, ' O delicious wound,' and so much the more delicious the more penetrating the fire of love. The Holy Ghost inflicted the wound that He might soothe it, and as His will and desire to soothe it are great, great will be the wound which He will inflict, in order that the soul He has wounded may be greatly comforted. O blessed wound inflicted by Him Who cannot but heal it !

9. O happy and most blessed wound ! For thou art inflicted only for the joy and comfort of the soul. Great is the wound, because He is great Who has wrought it ; and great is the delight of it : for the fire of love is infinite. O delicious wound then, and the more delicious the more the burn of love penetrates the inmost substance of the soul, burning all it can burn that it may supply all the delight it can give. This burning and wound, in my opinion, are the highest condition attainable in this life. There are many other forms of this burning, but they do not reach so far, neither are they like unto this : for this is the touch of the Divinity without form or figure, either natural, formal, or imaginary.

10. But the soul is burned in another and most excellent way, which is this : when a soul is on fire with love, but not in the degree of which I am now speaking— though it should be so, that it may be the subject of this —it will feel as if a seraph with a burning brand of love had struck it, and penetrated it already on fire as glowing coal, or rather as a flame, and burns it utterly.* And then in that burn the flame rushes forth and surges vehemently as in a glowing furnace or forge ; the fire revives and the flame ascends when the burning fuel is disturbed. Then when the burning brand touches it, the soul feels that the wound it has thus received is delicious beyond all imagination. For beside being altogether moved or stirred, at the time of this stirring of the fire, by the vehement movement of the seraph, wherein the ardour and the melting of love is great, it feels that its wound is perfect, and that the herbs which serve to attemper the steel are efficacious ; it feels the very depths of the spirit transpierced, and its delight to be exquisite beyond the power of language to express. The soul feels, as it were, a most minute grain of mustard seed, most pungent and burning in the inmost heart of the spirit ; in the spot of the wound, where the substance and the power of the herb reside, diffuse itself

* See *Life of the Teresa*, written by herself, xxix. 17 (transverberation of her heart).

most subtilely through all the spiritual veins of the soul in proportion to the strength and power of the heat. It feels its love to grow, strengthen, and refine itself to such a degree, as to seem to itself as if seas of fire were in it filling it with love.

11. The fruition of the soul now cannot be described otherwise than by saying that it understands why the kingdom of heaven is compared in the gospel to a mustard seed, which by reason of its great natural heat grows into a lofty tree. ' The kingdom of heaven is like a grain of mustard seed, which a man took and sowed in his field. Which is the least surely of all seeds ; but when it is grown up, it is greater than all herbs, and is made a tree, so that the fowls of the air come and dwell in the branches thereof.' * The soul beholds itself now as one immense sea of fire. Few souls, however, attain to this state, but some have done so, especially those whose spirit and power is to be transmitted to their spiritual children ; since God bestows on the founder gifts and graces, according to the succession of the order in the first-fruits of the Spirit.

12. To return to the work of the seraph, which in truth is to strike and wound. If the effect of the wound be permitted to flow exteriorly into the bodily senses, an effect corresponding to the interior wound itself will

* St. Matth. xiii. 31, 32.

manifest itself without. Thus it was with St. Francis, for when the seraph wounded his soul with love, the effects of that wound became outwardly visible. God confers no favours on the body which He does not confer in the first place chiefly on the soul. In that case, the greater the joy and violence of the love which is the cause of the interior wound, the greater will be the pain of the visible wound, and as the former grows so does the latter.

13. The reason is this : such souls as these, being already purified and strong in God, their spirit, strong and sound, delights in the strong and sweet Spirit of God ; Who, however, causes pain and suffering in their weak and corruptible flesh. It is thus a most marvellous thing to feel pain and sweetness together. Job felt it when he said, ' Returning, Thou tormentest me wonderfully.' * This is marvellous, worthy of the multitude of the sweetness of God, which He has hidden for them that fear Him ; † the greater the sweetness and delight, the greater the pain and suffering.

14. O Infinite greatness, in all things showing Thyself omnipotent. Who, O Lord, can cause sweetness in the midst of bitterness, and pleasure in the midst of pain ? O delicious wound, the greater the delight the deeper the wound. But when the wound is within

* Job x. 16.   † Ps. xxx. 20.

the soul, and not communicated to the body without, it is then much more intense and keen.   As the flesh is bridle to the spirit, so, when the graces of the latter overflow into the former, the flesh draws in and restrains the swift steed of the spirit and checks its course ; ' for the corruptible body is a load upon the soul, and the earthly habitation presseth down the mind that museth upon many things.' * He, therefore, who shall trust much to the bodily senses will never become a very spiritual man.

15.   This I say for the sake of those who think they can ascend to the heights and power of the spirit, by the mere energy and action of the senses, which are mean and vile.   We cannot become spiritual unless the bodily sense be restrained.   It is a state of things wholly different from this, when the spirit overflows into the senses, for there may be great spirituality in this ; as in the case of St. Paul, whose deep sense of the sufferings of Christ overflowed into his body, so that he said : ' I bear the marks of our Lord Jesus in my body.' †   Thus, as the wound and the burn, so the hand that inflicted it ; and as the touch, so He who touched.   ' O tender hand, O gentle touch.'

' O tender hand, O gentle touch.'

16.   O hand, as generous as Thou art powerful and

* Wisd. ix. 15.   † Gal. vi. 17.

rich, giving me gifts with power. O gentle hand! laid so gently upon me, and yet, if Thou wert to press at all, the whole world must perish ; for only at the sight of Thee the earth trembles,* the nations melt, and the mountains are crushed in pieces.† O gentle hand, I say it again, for him thou didst touch so sharply. Upon me Thou art laid so softly, so lovingly, and so tenderly ; Thou art the more gentle and sweet for me than thou wert hard for him ; the loving sweetness with which Thou art laid upon me is greater than the severity with which he was touched. Thou killest, and Thou givest life, and there is no one who shall escape out of Thy hand.

17. But Thou, O divine life, never killest but to give life, as Thou never woundest but to heal. Thou hast wounded me, O divine hand! that Thou mayest heal me. Thou hast slain in me that which made me dead, and without the life of God which I now live. This Thou hast wrought in the liberality of Thy gracious generosity, through that touch, wherewith Thou dost touch me, of the brightness of Thy glory and the figure of Thy substance,‡ Thine only begotten Son, in Whom being Thy Wisdom, Thou reachest ' from end to end mightily.' §

---

* Ps. ciii. 32. † Hab. iii. 6.
‡ Heb. i. 3. § Wisd. viii. 1.

18. O gentle, subtile touch, the Word, the Son of God, Who, because of the pureness of Thy divine nature, dost penetrate subtilely the very substance of my soul, and, touching it gently, absorbest it wholly in divine ways of sweetness not ' heard of in the land of Canaan,' nor ' seen in Teman.' * O touch of the Word, so gentle, so wonderfully gentle to me ; and yet Thou wert ' over-throwing mountains, and breaking rocks in Horeb,' by the shadow of Thy power going before, when Thou didst announce Thy presence to the prophet in ' the whisper of a gentle air.' † O soft air, how is it that Thou touchest so softly when Thou art so terrible and so strong ? O blessed soul, most blessed, which Thou, who art so terrible and so strong, touchest so gently. Proclaim it to the world, O my soul—no, proclaim it not, for the world knoweth not the ' gentle air,' neither will it listen to it, because it cannot comprehend matters so deep.

19. O my God and my life, they shall know Thee ‡ and behold Thee when Thou touchest them, who, making themselves strangers upon earth, shall purify themselves, because purity corresponds with purity. The more gently Thou touchest, the more Thou art hidden in the purified soul of those who have made themselves strangers here, hidden from the face of all creatures,

* Bar. iii. 22.   † 3 Kings xix. 11, 12.
‡ St. John xiv. 17.

and whom ' Thou shalt hide in the secret of Thy face from the disturbance of men.' *

20. O, again and again, gentle touch, which by the power of its tenderness, undoest the soul, removest it far away from every touch whatever, and makest it Thine own ; Thou which leavest behind Thee effects and impressions so pure, that the touch of everything else seems vile and low, the very sight offensive, and all relations therewith a deep affliction. The more subtile any matter is, the more it spreads and fills, and the more it diffuses itself the more subtile is it. O gentle touch, the more subtile the more infused. And now the vessel of my soul, because Thou hast touched it, is pure and clean and able to receive Thee.

21. O gentle touch ! as in Thee there is nothing material, so Thy touch is the more penetrating, changing what in me is human into divine, for Thy Divine essence, wherewith Thou touchest me, is wholly unaffected by modes and manner, free from the husks of form and figure. Finally then, O gentle touch, and most gentle, for Thou touchest me with Thy most simple and pure essence, which being infinite is infinitely gentle ; therefore it is that this touch is so subtile, so loving, so deep, and so delicious.

'Savouring of everlasting life.'

* Ps. xxx. 21.

22. What the soul tastes now in this touch of God, is, in truth, though not perfectly, a certain foretaste of everlasting life, as I said before.* It is not incredible that it should be so when we believe, as we do believe, that this touch is most substantial, and that the substance of God touches the substance of the soul. Many Saints have experienced it in this life. The sweetness of delight which this touch occasions baffles all description. Neither will I speak of it, lest men should suppose that it is nothing beyond what my words imply, for there are no terms by which we can designate or explain the deep things of God transacted in perfect souls. The proper way to speak of them is for him who has been favoured with them to understand them, feel them, and enjoy them, and be silent.

23. For the soul now sees that they are in some measure like the white counter of which it is written ' To him that overcometh I will give . . . a white counter, and in the counter a new name written, which no man knoweth but he that receiveth it.' † Thus it may be truly said, ' savouring of everlasting life.' For though the fruition of it is not perfect in this life as it will be in glory ; nevertheless the touch, being of God, savoureth of everlasting life, and accordingly the soul tastes in a marvellous manner, and by participation,

* Stanza i. 7.   † Apoc. ii. 17.

of all the things of God ; fortitude, wisdom, love, beauty, grace, and goodness being communicated unto it.

24. Now as God is all this, the soul tastes of all in one single touch of God in a certain eminent way. And from this good bestowed upon the soul, some of the unction of the Spirit overflows at times into the body itself, penetrating into the very bones, as it is written, ' All my bones shall say : Lord, who is like unto Thee ? ' * But as all I can say falls short of the subject, it is enough to repeat, ' savouring of everlasting life.'

' And paying the whole debt.'

25. But what debts are they to which the soul here refers, and which it declares to be paid or satisfied ? We should know that souls which attain to this high state, to the kingdom of the spiritual betrothal, have in general passed through many tribulations and trials, because it is ' through many tribulations that we enter into the kingdom of heaven.' † And these tribulations are now passed.

26. What they have to suffer who are to attain unto union with God, are divers afflictions and temptations of sense, trials, tribulations, temptations, darkness, and distress of mind, so that both the flesh and the spirit may be purified together, as I said in the *Dark Night*

* Ps. xxxiv. 10.   † Acts xiv. 21.

in my treatise of the *Ascent of Mount Carmel*. The reason is that the joy and knowledge of God cannot be established in the soul, if the flesh and spirit are not perfectly purified and spiritualised, and as trials and penances purify and refine the senses, as tribulations, temptations, darkness and distress spiritualise and prepare the spirit, so they must undergo them who would be transformed in God—as the souls in purgatory who through that trial attain to the beatific vision—some more intensely than others, some for a longer, others for a shorter time, according to those degrees of union to which God intends to raise them, and according to their need of purification.

27. It is by these trials to which God subjects the spirit and the flesh that the soul, in bitterness, acquires virtues and fortitude and perfection, as the Apostle writes, ' Power is made perfect in infirmity ; ' * for virtue is made perfect in weakness, and refined by sufferings. Iron cannot be fashioned according to the pattern of the artificer but by fire and the hammer, and during the process its previous condition is injured. This is the way in which God taught Jeremias, ' From on high He hath cast a fire in my bones and hath taught me.' †
The prophet speaks of the hammer also when he saith, ' Thou hast chastised me, and I am taught.' ‡   So, too,

* 2 Cor. xii. 9.   † Lam. i. 13.   ‡ Jerem. xxxi. 18.

the Wise Man asks, ' He that hath not been proved, what knoweth he ? ' *

28. Here comes the question, why is it that so few ever attain to this state ? The reason is that, in this marvellous work which God Himself begins, so many are weak, shrinking from trouble, and unwilling to endure the least discomfort or mortification, or to labour with constant patience. Hence it is that God, not finding them diligent in cultivating the graces He has given them when He began to try them, proceeds no further with their purification, neither does He lift them up out of the dust of the earth, because it required greater courage and resolution for this than they possessed.

29. Thus it may be said to those who desire to advance, but who will not endure a lighter trial nor submit themselves thereto, in the words of Jeremias, ' If with running with footmen thou hast laboured how canst thou contend with horses ? and whereas in a land of peace thou hast been secure, what wilt thou do in the pride of Jordan ? ' † That is, if the ordinary trials of human life to which all men living are liable are wearisome and a burden for thee, how art thou to ' contend with horses ' ? that is, how canst thou venture out of the common trials of life upon others of greater violence and swiftness ? If thou hast been unwilling

* Ecclus. xxxiv. 11   † Jerem. xii. 5.

to make war against the peace and pleasures of the
earth, thine own sensuality, but rather seekest comfort
and tranquillity on it, what wilt thou do in the pride
of Jordan ? that is, how wilt thou stand against the
rushing waters of tribulations and the more interior
trials of the spirit ?

30. O souls that seek your own ease and comfort, if
you knew how necessary for this high state is suffering,
and how profitable suffering and mortification are for
attaining to these great blessings, you would never seek
for comfort anywhere, but you would rather take up the
cross with the vinegar and the gall, and would count
it an inestimable favour, knowing that by thus dying
to the world and to your own selves, you would live to
God in spiritual joy ; in the patient endurance of your
exterior afflictions you would merit at the hands of God,
that He should look upon you, cleanse and purify you more
and more in these spiritual tribulations.   They whom He
thus blesses must have served Him well and long, must
have been patient and persevering, and their life most
pleasing in His sight.   The angel said unto Tobias
' Because thou wast acceptable to God, it was necessary
that temptation should prove thee.' *   Tobias was
acceptable to God, therefore He tried him ; He gave him
the grace of tribulation, the source of greater graces

* Tob. xii. 13.

still, and it is written of him that ' the rest of his life was in joy.' *

31. The same truth is exemplified in the life of Job. God acknowledged him as His faithful servant in the presence of the angels good and evil, and immediately sent him heavy trials, that He might afterwards raise him higher, as He did, both in temporal and spiritual things.†

32. This is the way God deals with those whom it is His will to exalt. He suffers them to be tempted, afflicted, tormented and chastened, inwardly and outwardly, to the utmost limit of their strength, that He may deify them, unite them to Himself in His wisdom, which is the highest state, purifying them, first in that wisdom, as David observed, saying that the ' words of our Lord are chaste words, silver, examined by fire,' tested in the earth of our flesh and purified ‡ seven times, that is, made perfectly pure.

33. It is not necessary I should stop here to say how each of these purgations tends to the divine wisdom, which in this life is as silver, for however pure it may be, yet is not comparable to the pure gold, which is reserved for everlasting glory.

34. But it is very necessary for the soul to endure these tribulations and trials, inward and outward,

---

* Tob. xiv. 4.   † Job i. 8–20.   ‡ Ps. xi. 7.

spiritual and corporal, great and small, with great resolution and patience, accepting all as from the hand of
God for its healing and its good, not shrinking from
them, because they are for the health of the soul. ' If
the spirit of him that hath power,' saith the Wise Man,
' ascend upon thee, leave not thy place, because carefulness '—that is healing—' will make the greatest sins to
cease.' * ' Leave not thy place,' that is, the place of thy
trial, which is thy troubles ; for the healing which they
bring will break the thread of thy sins and imperfections,
which is evil habits, so that they shall proceed no further.
Thus, interior trials and tribulations destroy and purge
away the imperfect and evil habits of the soul. We
are, therefore, to count it a great favour when our Lord
sends us interior and exterior trials, remembering that
they are few in number who deserve to be made perfect
through sufferings so as to attain to so high a state
as this.

35. I return to the explanation of the words before
me. The soul now remembers that its past afflictions
are most abundantly recompensed, for ' as the darkness
so also the light thereof,' † and that having once been
' a partaker of the sufferings,' it is now ' of the consolation,' ‡ that its interior and exterior trials have been
recompensed by the divine mercies, none of them being

* Eccles. x. 4. † Ps. cxxxviii. 12. ‡ 2 Cor. i. 7.

without its corresponding reward. It therefore acknowledges itself perfectly satisfied, and says, ' paying the whole debt,' as David did, ' How great tribulations hast Thou shown me, many and evil, and turning Thou hast quickened me, and from the depths of the earth Thou hast brought me back again. Thou hast multiplied Thy magnificence, and turning to me Thou hast comforted me.' *

36. Thus the soul which once stood without at the gates of the palace of God—like Mardochai weeping in the streets of Susan because his life was threatened, clothed with sackcloth and refusing the garments which Esther sent him, unrewarded for his faithful service in defending the king's honour and life,†—finds, also, like Mardochai, all its trials and service rewarded in one day. It is not only admitted within the palace and stands in royal robes before the king, but has also a diadem on its head, and in its hand a sceptre, and sitting on the royal throne with the king's signet on its finger, symbols of its power in the kingdom of the Bridegroom. For those souls who attain to this high state obtain all their desires ; the whole debt is amply paid : the appetites, their enemies which sought their life, are dead, while they are living in God. ' In destroying death Thou hast changed it into life.'

* Ps. lxx. 20.   † Esth. iv. 1-6.

' Thou hast changed death into life.'

37. Death is nothing else but the privation of life,
for when life cometh there is no trace of death in that
which is spiritual. There are two kinds of life, one
beatific, consisting in the vision of God, and this must
be preceded by a natural and bodily death, as it is written,
' We know if our earthly house of this habitation be dissolved, that we have a building of God, a house not made
with hands, eternal in heaven.' *   The other is the perfect
spiritual life, consisting in the possession of God by the
union of love.   Men attain to this through the mortification of their evil habits and desires.   Until this be
done, the perfection of the spiritual life of union with
God is unattainable, ' For,' as the Apostle saith, ' if you
live according to the flesh, you shall die : but if by the
spirit you mortify the deeds of the flesh, you shall live.' †

38. By ' death ' here is meant the old man, that is
the employment of our faculties, memory, understanding,
and will, upon the things of this world, and the desire on
the pleasure which created things supply.   All this is the
old life ; it is the death of the new life which is spiritual,
and which the soul cannot live perfectly unless to the old
man it be perfectly dead, for so the Apostle teaches, when
he bids us put ' away according to the old conversation,
the old man . . . and put on the new man, which, accord-

* 2 Cor. v. 1.   † Rom. viii. 13.

ing to God, is created in justice and holiness of the truth.' *
In this new life, when the soul shall have attained
to perfect union with God, all its affections, powers,
and acts, in themselves imperfect and vile, become as
it were divine. And as everything that lives, to use the
expression of philosophers, lives in its acts, so the soul,
having its acts in God by virtue of its union with Him,
lives the life of God, its death being changed into life.

39. This is so, because the understanding, which,
previous to its union with God, understood but dimly by
means of its natural light, is now under the influence and
direction of another principle, and of a higher illumination
of God. The will, which previously loved but weakly, is
now changed into the life of divine love, for now it loves
deeply with the affections of divine love, moved by the
Holy Ghost in whom it now lives. The memory, which
once saw nothing but the forms and figures of created
things, is now changed, and keeps in ' mind the eternal
years,'† as David spoke. The desire, which previously
longed for created food, now tastes and relishes the food
that is divine, influenced by another and more efficacious
principle, the sweetness of God.

40. Finally, all the motions and acts of the soul.
proceeding from the principle of its natural and imperfect
life, are now changed in this union with God into motions

* Ephes. iv. 22, 24.   † Ps. lxxvi. 6.

divine. For the soul, as the true child of God, is moved by the Spirit of God, as it is written, ' Whosoever are led by the Spirit of God, they are the sons of God.' * The substance of the soul, though it is not the substance of God, because inconvertible into Him, yet being united to Him and absorbed in Him, is by participation God. This is accomplished in the perfect state of the spiritual life, but not so perfectly as in the other ; hence is it well said : ' While slaying thou hast changed death into life.'

41. The soul, therefore, has good reason for saying with St. Paul, ' I live, now not I, but Christ liveth in me.' † What in the soul is dead and cold, becomes changed into the life of God, the soul ' swallowed up of life ' ‡ in fulfilling the words of the Apostle, ' Death is swallowed up in victory,' § and those of Osee, ' I will be thy death, O death.' ||

42. The soul being thus swallowed up of life, detached from all secular and temporal things, and delivered from the disorderliness of nature, is led into the chamber of the King, where it rejoices and is glad in the Beloved, remembering His breasts more than wine, and saying, ' I am black but beautiful, O ye daughters of Jerusalem,' ¶ for my natural blackness is changed into the beauty of the heavenly King. O then, the burning of the fire !

---

* Rom. viii. 14.   † Gal. ii. 20.   ‡ 2 Cor. v. 4.
§ 1 Cor. xv. 54. || Os. xiii. 14.   ¶ Cant. i. 4.

infinitely burning above all other fires, O how infinitely beyond all other fires dost thou burn me, and the more thou burnest the sweeter thou art to me. ' O delicious wound,' more delicious to me than all the delights and health of the world. ' O tender hand,' infinitely more tender than all tenderness, and the greater the pressure of it the more tender is it to me. ' O gentle touch,' the gentleness of which surpasses infinitely all the gentleness and all the loveliness of created things, sweeter and more delicious than honey and the honeycomb, because thou savourest of everlasting life ; and is the more sweet the more profoundly thou dost touch me. Thou art infinitely more precious than gold and precious stones, for thou payest debts which nothing else can pay, because thou changest marvellously death into life.

43. In this state of life, so perfect, the soul is, as it were, keeping a perpetual feast with the praises of God in its mouth, with a new song of joy and love, full of the knowledge of its high dignity. It sometimes exulteth, repeating the words of Job, ' My glory shall always be renewed,' and ' as a palm tree ' I ' will multiply days.' * That is, God will not suffer my glory to grow old as before, and He will multiply my days, that is, my merits, unto heaven, as a palm tree multiplies its branches. And also the words of David in the twenty-ninth Psalm, the

* Job xxix. 18, 20.

soul sings interiorly to God, especially the conclusion thereof, ' Thou hast turned my mourning into joy unto me : Thou hast cut my sackcloth and hast compassed me with gladness, that my glory may sing to Thee, and I be not compunct '—for this state is inaccessible to pain— ' Lord my God, for ever will I confess to Thee.' *

44.   Here the soul is so conscious of God's solicitude to comfort it, feeling that He is Himself encouraging it with words so precious, so tender, so endearing ; that He is conferring graces upon it, one upon another, so that it seems as if there were no other soul in the world for Him to comfort, no other object of His care, but that everything was done for this one soul alone.   This truth is admitted by the bride in the Canticle when she says, ' My Beloved to me and I to Him.' †

STANZA III

O lamps of fire,
In the splendours of which
The deep caverns of sense,
Dim and dark
With unwonted brightness
Give light and warmth together to their Beloved.

EXPLANATION

I STAND greatly in need of the help of God to enter into the deep meaning of this stanza : great attention also is

* Ps. xxix. 12, 13.   † Cant. ii, 16.

necessary on the part of the reader, for if he be without experience of the matter he will find it very obscure, while, on the other hand, it will be clear and full of sweetness to him who has had that experience.

2. In this stanza the soul most heartily thanks the Bridegroom for the great mercies which, in the state of union, it has received at His hands, for He has given therein a manifold and most profound knowledge of Himself, which enlightens its powers and senses, and fills them with love. These powers, previous to the state of union, were in darkness and blindness, but are now illumined by the fires of love and respond thereto, offering that very light and love to Him who has kindled and inspired them by infusing into the soul gifts so divine. For he who truly loves is satisfied then when his whole self, all he is, all he can be, all he has, and all he can acquire, is spent in the service of his love ; and the greater that service the greater is his pleasure in giving it. Such is the joy of the soul now, because it can shine in the presence of the Beloved in the splendours with which He has surrounded it, and love Him with that love which He has communicated to it.

'O Lamps of fire.'

3. Lamps have two properties, that of giving light and of burning. If we are to understand this stanza, we must keep in mind, that God in His one and simple essence is

all the power and majesty of His attributes. He is omnipotent, wise, good, merciful, just, strong, loving ; He is all the other attributes and perfections of which we have no knowledge here below. He is all this. When the soul is in union with Him, and He is pleased to admit it to a special knowledge of Himself, the soul sees in Him all these perfections and majesty together in the one and simple essence clearly and distinctly, so far as it is consistent with the faith, and as each one of these attributes is the very being of God, Who is the Father, the Son, and the Holy Ghost—as each attribute is God Himself—and as God is infinite light, and infinite divine fire, it follows that each attribute gives light and burns as God Himself. God therefore, according to this knowledge of Him in unity, is to the soul as many lamps, because it has the knowledge of each of them, and because they minister to it the warmth of love, each in its own way, and yet all of one substance, all one lamp. This lamp is all lamps, because it gives light, and burns, in all ways.

4. The soul seeing this, the one lamp is to it as many lamps, for though but one, it can do all things, and has all power and comprehends every spirit. And thus it may be said that the one lamp shines and burns many ways in one : it shines and burns as omnipotent, as wise, as good, ministering to the soul knowledge and love, and revealing itself unto it, according to the measure of its

strength for the reception of all. The splendour of the lamp as omnipotent gives to the soul the light and warmth of the love of God as omnipotent, and accordingly God is now the lamp of omnipotence to the soul, shining and burning according to that attribute. The splendour of the lamp as wisdom produces the warmth of the love of God as all wise, and so of the other attributes ; for the light which emanates from each of the attributes of God and from all the others, produces in the soul the fire of the love of God as such. Thus God is to the soul in these communications and manifestations of Himself—they are, I think, the highest possible in this life—as innumerable lamps from which light and love proceed.

5. These lamps revealed Him to Moses on Mount Sinai, where God passed before Him, and where Moses fell prostrate on the earth in all haste. He mentions some of the perfections of God which he then saw, and, loving Him in them, speaks of them separately in the following words : ' O Lord God, merciful and clement, patient and of much compassion, and true, Who keepest mercy unto thousands ; Who takest away iniquity and wicked deeds and sin, and no man of himself is innocent before Thee.' * It appears that the principal attributes of God which Moses then recognised and loved were those of omnipotence, dominion, mercy, justice and truth

* Exod. xxxiv. 6, 7.

which was a most profound knowledge, and the deepest delight of love.

6. It follows from this that the joy and rapture of love communicated to the soul in the fire of the light of these lamps is admirable, and immeasurable : as abundant as from many lamps, each of which burns with love, the heat of one subserving that of the other, as the light of one ministers to that of the other ; all of them forming but one light and fire, and each of them that one fire. The soul, too, infinitely absorbed in these delicious flames, is subtilely wounded by each one of them, and by all of them more subtilely and more profoundly, in the love of life ; the soul sees clearly that this love is everlasting life, which is the union of all blessings, and recognises the truth of those words, ' The lamps thereof lamps of fire and flames.' *

7. If ' a great and darksome horror seized upon ' Abram as he saw one ' lamp of fire passing ' † before him, when he learned with what rigorous justice God was about to visit the Chananeans, shall not the lamps of the knowledge of God shining now sweetly and lovingly produce greater light and joy of love than that one lamp produced of horror and darkness, when it passed before Abram ? O my soul ! how great, how excellent, and how manifold, will be thy light and joy :

* Cant. viii. 6.   † Gen. xv. 12, 17.

seeing that in all, and by all, thou shalt feel that He gives thee His own joy and love, loving thee according to His powers, attributes, and properties. For he who loves and does good to another honours him and does him good according to his own nature and qualities. Thus the Bridegroom abiding in thee, being all-powerful, gives Himself to thee, and loves thee with all power ; being wise, with wisdom ; being good, with goodness ; being holy, with holiness. And as He is liberal thou wilt feel also that He loves thee with liberality, without self-interest, only to do thee good, showing joyfully His countenance full of grace, and saying : I am thine and for thee, and it is My pleasure to be what I am, that I may give Myself to thee and be thine.

8. Who then shall describe thy feeling, O blessed soul, when thus beloved, and so highly honoured ? ' Thy belly as a heap of wheat compassed about with lilies.' * ' Thy belly,' that is, thy will, is like a heap of wheat covered and compassed with lilies ; for in the grains of wheat which form the bread of life, which thou now art tasting, the lilies of virtue, which gird thee about, fill thee with delight. For the daughters of the king, that is the virtues, will delight thee wondrously with the fragrance of their aromatical herbs, which are

* Cant. vii. 2.

the knowledge of Himself which He gives thee. Thou wilt be so absorbed in this knowledge, and it will be so infused in thee, that thou shalt be also ' a well of living waters which run with a strong stream from Mount Libanus,' * and Libanus is God. Thy joy will now be so marvellously complete, because the words of the Psalmist are accomplished in thee : ' The violence of the river maketh the city of God joyful.' †

9. O wonder ! The soul is now overflowing with the divine waters, which run from it as from an abundant fountain unto everlasting life.‡ It is true that this communication is light and fire of the lamps of God, yet the fire is here so sweet, that though an infinite fire, it is as the waters of life which satisfy the soul, and quench its thirst with that vehemence for which the spirit longs. Thus, though they are lamps of fire, they are also the living waters of the spirit. Those which descended on the Apostles, though lamps of fire, were also waters pure and limpid, according to the words of Ezechiel who thus prophesied the descent of the Holy Ghost : ' I will pour out upon you clean water, and will put a new spirit in the midst of you.' § Thus though it be fire, it is water also, a figure of which we have in the sacrificial fire, hid by Jeremias,‖ it was water in the place of concealment,

---

* Cant. iv. 15.   † Ps. xlv. 5.   ‡ St. John iv. 14.
§ Ezech. xxxvi. 25, 26.   ‖ 2 Mac. ii. 1.

but fire when it was brought forth and sprinkled upon the sacrifice.*

10. So in like manner the Spirit of God, while hidden in the veins of the soul, is sweet water quenching its spiritual thirst ; but when the soul offers the sacrifice of love, the Spirit is then living flames of fire, and these are the lamps of the acts of love which the bride spoke of in the Canticle when she said, ' The lamps thereof lamps of fire and flames.' † The soul speaks of them thus because it has the fruition thereof not only as waters of wisdom, but also as the fire of love in an act of love, saying, ' O lamps of fire.' All language now is ineffectual to express the matter. If we consider that the soul is now transformed in God, we shall in some measure understand how it is true that it is also become a fountain of living waters boiling and bubbling upwards in the fire of love which is God.

' In the splendours.'

11. I have already said that these splendours are the communications of the divine lamps in which the soul in union shines with its powers, memory, understanding, and will, enlightened and united in this loving knowledge. But we are not to suppose that the light of these splendours is like that of material fire, when it breaks into flames and heats objects external to it, but

* 2 Mac. i. 22.   † Cant. viii. 6.

rather when it heats what is within it, for the soul is now within these splendours—' in the splendours.' That is to say, it is within them, nor near them, within their splendours, in the flames of the lamps, itself transformed in flame.

12. The soul therefore may be said to resemble the air which is burning within the flame and transformed in fire, for the flame is nothing else but air inflamed. The flickerings of the flame are not those of air only or of fire only, but of air and fire together ; and the fire causes the air which is within to burn. It is thus that the soul with its powers is illumined in the splendours of God. The movements of the flame, that is its vibrations and its flickerings, are not the work of the soul only, transformed in the fire of the Holy Ghost, nor of the Holy Ghost only, but of the soul and of the Holy Ghost together Who moves the soul as the fire moves the air that is burning.

13. Thus, then, these movements of God and of the soul together are as it were the acts of God by which He renders the soul glorious. For these vibrations and movements are the ' playing ' and the joyous feasts of the Holy Ghost in the soul, spoken of before,* in which He seems to be on the point of admitting it into ever-lasting life. And thus these movements and quiverings

* Stanza I., 10 (line 2).

of the flame are as it were goads applied to the soul, furthering its translation into His perfect glory now that it is really entered into Him.   So with fire : all movements and vibrations which it makes in the air burning within it, are efforts to ascend to its proper sphere, and that as quickly as possible, but they are all fruitless because the air itself is within its own sphere.

14.   In the same way the movements of the Holy Ghost, though full of fire and most effectual to absorb the soul in great bliss, do not accomplish their work until the time is come when it is to sally forth from the sphere of the air of this mortal life and reach the centre of the spirit, the perfect life in Christ.   These visions of the glory of God, to which the soul is now admitted, are more continuous than they used to be, more perfect and more stable ; but in the life to come they will be most perfect, unchanging, and uninterrupted.   There, too, the soul will see clearly how that God, though here appearing to move within it, yet in Himself moves not at all, as the fire moves not in its sphere.   These splendours are inestimable graces and favours which God bestows upon the soul.   They are called also overshadowings, and are, in my opinion, the greatest and the highest graces which can be bestowed in this life in the way of transformation.

15.   Now overshadowing is the throwing of a shadow ;

5

and to throw one's shadow over another signifies protection and favour, for when the shadow of one touches
us, it is a sign that he whose shadow it is stands by us to
favour and protect us. Thus it was said to the Virgin,
' The power of the Most High shall overshadow thee,' *
for the Holy Ghost was about to approach her so closely
as to ' come upon ' her. The shadow of every object
partakes of the nature and proportions of it, for if the
object be dense, the shadow will be dense and dark ; if it
be light and clear, so will be the shadow, as we see in the
case of wood or crystal : the former being dense, throws
a dark shadow, and the latter being clear, throws a
shadow that is light. In spiritual things, too, death is
the privation of all things, so the shadow of death will
be darkness, which in a manner deprives us of all things.
Thus, too, speaks the Psalmist, saying, ' sitting in darkness and the shadow of death,' † whether the spiritual
darkness of spiritual death, or the bodily darkness of
bodily death.

16. The shadow of life is light, if divine, a divine
light, and if the shadow be human, the light is natural,
and so the shadow of beauty will be as another beauty
according to the nature and properties of that beauty
of which it is the shadow. The shadow of strength will
be as another strength, in measure and proportion.

* St. Luke i. 35.   † Ps. cvi. 10.

The shadow of wisdom will be another wisdom, or rather, beauty, strength, and wisdom themselves will be in the shadow, wherein is traced the form and property, the shadow whereof is there.

17. This, then, being so, what must be the shadow of the Holy Ghost, the shadow of all His power, might, and attributes, when He is so near the soul ? He touches the soul not with His shadow only, for He unites Himself to it, feeling and tasting with it the form and attributes of God in the shadow of God : that is, feeling and tasting the property of divine power in the shadow of omnipotence : feeling and tasting the divine wisdom in the shadow of the divine wisdom : and finally, tasting the glory of God in the shadow of glory, which begets the knowledge and the taste of the property and form of the glory of God. All this takes place in clear and luminous shadows, because the attributes and powers of God are lamps, which, being resplendent and luminous in their own nature, throw forth shadows resplendent and luminous, and a multitude of them in one sole essence.

18. O what a vision for the soul when it shall experience the power of that which Ezechiel saw : ' the likeness of four living creatures,' and the ' wheel with four faces,' the appearance ' like that of burning coals of fire, and like the appearance of lamps ; ' * when it

* Ezech. i. 5, 13, 15,

shall behold that wheel, the wisdom of God, full of eyes within and without, that is the marvellous knowledge of wisdom ; when it shall hear the noise of their wings as they pass, a noise ' like the noise of an army,' that is of many things at once which the soul learns by one sole sound of God's passing before it ; and finally, when it shall hear the beating of the wings, which is like the ' noise of many waters, as it were the voice of the Most High God,' * which signifies the rushing of the divine waters, the overflowing of which on the descent of the Holy Ghost envelopes the soul in a flame of love. Here the soul rejoices in the glory of God, under the protection of His shadow, for the prophet adds : ' This was the vision of the likeness of the glory of our Lord.' †
O the height to which this blessed soul is raised ! O how exalted ! O how it marvels at the visions it has within the limits of the faith ! Who can describe them ? O how it is profoundly immersed in these waters of the divine splendours where the everlasting Father is pouring forth the irrigating streams with a bounteous hand, for these streams penetrate soul and body.

19. O wonder ! the lamps of the divine attributes, though one in substance, are still distinct, each burning as the other, one being substantially the other. O abyss of delights, and the more abundant, the more

* Ezech. i. 24.   † Ib. ii. 1.

their riches are gathered together in infinite simplicity and unity. There each one is so recognised and felt as not to hinder the feeling and recognition of the other ; yea, rather everything in Thee is light which does not impede anything ; and by reason of Thy pureness, O divine Wisdom, many things are known in Thee in one, for Thou art the treasury of the everlasting Father, ' the brightness of eternal light, the unspotted mirror of God's majesty, and the image of His goodness,' * ' in the splendours.'

' The deep caverns of sense.'

20. The caverns are the powers of the soul, memory, understanding, and will, and their depth is commensurate with their capacity for great good, because nothing less than the infinite can fill them. What they suffer when they are empty, shows in some measure the greatness of their delight when they are full of God ; for contraries are known by contraries. In the first place, it is to be remembered that these caverns are not conscious of their extreme emptiness when they are not purified and cleansed from all affection for created things. In this life every trifle that enters them is enough to perplex them, to render them insensible to their loss, and unable to recognise the infinite good which is wanting, or their own capacity for it. It is

* Wisd. vii. 26.

assuredly a most wonderful thing how, notwithstanding their capacity for infinite good, a mere trifle perplexes them, so that they cannot become the recipients of that for which they are intended, till they are completely emptied.

21. But when they are empty and cleansed, the hunger, the thirst, and the anxiety of the spiritual sense become intolerable, for as the appetite of these caverns is large, so their suffering is great, because the food which they need is great, namely, God. This feeling of pain, so deep, usually occurs towards the close of the illumination and the purgation of the soul, previous to the state of perfect union, during which it is satisfied. For when the spiritual appetite is empty, pure from every creature and from every affection thereto, and when the natural temper is lost and the soul attempered to the divine, and the emptied appetite is well disposed —the divine communication in the union with God being still withheld—the pain of this emptiness and thirst is greater than that of death, especially then when certain glimpses of the divine ray are visible, but not communicated. Souls in this state suffer from impatient love, and they cannot endure it long without either receiving that which they desire, or dying.' *

22. As to the first cavern, which is the understand-

* See *Spirit. Cant.*, Stanza vii. 3.

ing, its emptiness is the thirst after God. So great is this thirst, that the Psalmist compares it to that of the hart, for he knew of none greater, saying, ' As the hart desireth the fountains of waters : so doth my soul desire Thee, O God.' * This thirst is a thirst for the waters of the divine Wisdom, the object of the understanding. The second cavern is the will, and the emptiness thereof is a hunger so great after God, that the soul faints away, as the Psalmist saith, ' My soul longeth and fainteth for the courts of our Lord.' † This hunger is for the perfection of love, the object of the soul's desires. The third cavern is the memory, and the emptiness thereof is the soul's melting away and languishing for the possession of God : ' I will be mindful and remember,' saith Jeremias, ' and my soul shall languish within me : these things I shall think over in my heart, therefore will I hope.' ‡

23. Great, then, is the capacity of these caverns, because that which they are capable of containing is great and infinite, that is, God. Thus their capacity is in a certain sense infinite, their hunger and thirst infinite also, and their languishing and their pain, in their way, infinite. So when the soul is suffering this pain, though the pain be not so keen as in the other world, it seems

---

* Ps. xli. 2.   † *Ib.* lxxxiii. 3.
‡ Lam. iii. 20, 21.

to be a vivid image of that pain, because the soul is in a measure prepared to receive that which fills it, the privation of which is the greatest pain. Nevertheless the suffering belongs to another condition, for it abides in the depth of the will's love ; but in this life love does not alleviate the pain, because the greater it is the greater the soul's impatience for the fruition of God, for which it hopes continually with intense desire.

24. But, O my God, seeing it is certain that when the soul truly longs for God it is already, as St. Gregory saith,* entered into possession, how comes it that it is in pain ? If the desire of the angels, of which St. Peter speaks, to look upon the Son of God † is free from pain and anxiety, because they have the fruition of Him, it would seem then that the soul also having the fruition of God in proportion to its desire of Him—and the fruition of God is the fulness of delight—must in this its desire, in proportion to its intensity, be conscious of that fulness, seeing that it longs so earnestly after God, and so herein there ought not to be any suffering or pain.

25. But it is not so, for there is a great difference between the fruition of God by grace only, and the fruition of Him in union ; the former is one of mutual

* 'Qui ergo mente integra Deum desiderat, profecto jam habet quem amat.'—Hom. 30 in *Evangel.*   † 1 St. Pet. i. 12.

good will, the latter one of special communion. This difference resembles that which exists between betrothal and marriage. The former implies only an agreement and consent ; bridal presents, and ornaments graciously given by the bridegroom. But marriage involves also personal union and mutual self-surrender. Though in the state of betrothal, the bridegroom is sometimes seen by the bride, and gives her presents ; yet there is no personal union, which is the end of betrothal.*

26. In the same way, when the soul has become so pure in itself, and in its powers, that the will is purged completely from all strange desires and inclinations, in its higher and lower nature, and is wholly given up to God, the will of both being one in free and ready concord, it has then attained to the fruition of God by grace in the state of betrothal and conformity of will. In this state of spiritual betrothal of the soul and the Word, the Bridegroom confers great favours upon the soul, and visits it oftentimes most lovingly to its great comfort and delight, but not to be compared with those of the spiritual marriage.

27. Now, though it is true that this takes place in the soul when it is perfectly cleansed of every affection to creatures—because that must occur previous to the spiritual betrothal—still other positive dispositions on

* St. Teresa, *Interior Castle*, V Mansion, iv. 1, 2 ; VII Mansion, ii. 2.

the part of God, His visits and gifts of greater excellence, are requisite for this union, and for the spiritual marriage. It is by means of these dispositions, gifts, and visits, that the soul grows more and more in purity, beauty, and refinement, so as to be meetly prepared for a union so high. All this requires time, in some souls more, in others less. We have a type of this in the history of the virgins chosen for king Assuerus. These were taken in all the provinces of the kingdom, and brought from their fathers' houses ; but before they could be presented to the king, they were kept in the palace a whole year. For six months they were anointed with oil of myrrh, and for the other six with certain perfumes and sweet spices of a costlier nature, after which they appeared in the presence of the king.*

28. During the time of the betrothal, and in expectation of the spiritual marriage in the unction of the Holy Ghost, when the unction disposing the soul for union is most penetrating, the anxieties of the caverns are wont to become most pressing and keen. For as these unctions are a proximate disposition for union with God, because most near unto Him, they make the soul more eager for Him, and inspire it with a keener longing after Him. Thus this desire is much more keen

* Esth. ii. 2, 12.

and deep, because the desire for God is a preparation for union with Him.

29. This is a good opportunity to warn souls whom God is guiding to this delicate unction to take care what they are doing, and to whose hands they commit themselves, that they may not go backwards, were it not beside my purpose. But such is the pain and grief of heart which I feel at the sight of some souls who go backwards, not only by withdrawing themselves from the further anointing of the Holy Ghost, but by losing the effects of what they have already received, that I cannot refrain from speaking on the subject, and telling them what they ought to do in order to avoid so great a loss. I will therefore leave my subject for a moment, but I shall return to it soon again. And in truth the consideration of this matter tends to elucidate the property of these caverns, and it is also necessary, not only for those souls who prosper in their work, but also for all others who are searching after the Beloved.

30. In the first place, if a soul is seeking after God, the Beloved is seeking it much more ; if it sends after Him its loving desires, which are sweet as ' a pillar of smoke of aromatical spices, of myrrh and frankincense,' * He on His part sends forth the odour of His ointments, which draw the soul and make it run after

* Cant. iii. 6.

Him.* These ointments are His divine inspirations and touches, which if they come from Him, are always directed and ordered by the motives of perfection according to the law of God and the faith, in which perfection the soul must ever draw nearer and nearer unto God. The soul, therefore, ought to see that the desire of God in all the graces which He bestows upon it by means of the unction and odour of His ointments, is to dispose it for another and higher unction, and more in union with His nature, until it attains to that simple and pure disposition, which is meritorious of the divine union, and of its transformation in all its powers.

31. The soul, therefore, considering that God is the chief doer in this matter, that it is He Who guides it and leads it by the hand whither it cannot come of itself, namely, unto supernatural things beyond the reach of understanding, memory, and will, must take especial care to put no difficulties in the way of its guide, Who is the Holy Ghost, on that road along which He leads it by the law of God and the faith. Such a difficulty will be raised if the soul intrusts itself to a blind guide ; and the blind guides which can lead it astray are three, namely, the spiritual director, the devil, and its own self.

* Cant. i. 3.

32. As to the first of these, it is of the greatest importance to the soul desirous of perfection and anxious not to fall back, to consider well into whose hands it resigns itself ; for as the master so is the disciple ; as the father so the child. You will scarcely find one who is in all respects qualified to guide a soul in the higher parts of this road, or even in the ordinary divisions of it, for a director must be learned, prudent and experienced. Though the foundations of good direction be learning and discretion, yet if experience of the higher ways be wanting, there are no means of guiding a soul therein when God is showing the way, and inexperienced directors may do great harm. Such directors, not understanding these ways of the Spirit, very frequently make souls lose the unction of the delicate ointments, by means of which the Holy Ghost is preparing them for Himself : they are guiding them by other means of which they have read, but which are adapted only for beginners. These directors, knowing how to guide beginners only—and God grant they may know that— will not suffer their penitents to advance, though it be the will of God, beyond the mere rudiments, acts of reflection and imagination, whereby their progress is extremely little.*

33. In order to have a better knowledge of the state

* St. Teresa, *Life*, ch. xiii. *passim*; *Way of Perfection*, v. 1, 2.

of beginners, we must keep in mind that it is one of meditation and of acts of reflection. It is necessary to furnish the soul in this state with matter for meditation, that it may make reflections and interior acts, and avail itself of the sensible spiritual heat and fervour, for this is necessary in order to accustom the senses and desires to good things, that, being satisfied by the sweetness thereof, they may be detached from the world.

34. When this is in some degree effected, God begins at once to introduce the soul into the state of contemplation, and that very quickly, especially religious, because these, having renounced the world, quickly fashion their senses and desires according to God ; they have therefore to pass at once from meditation to contemplation. This passage, then, takes place when the discursive acts and meditation fail, when sensible sweetness and first fervours cease, when the soul cannot make reflections as before, nor find any sensible comfort, but is fallen into aridity, because the chief matter is changed into the spirit, and the spirit is not cognisable by sense. As all the natural operations of the soul, which are within its control, depend on the senses only, it follows that God is now working in a special manner in this state, that it is He that infuses and teaches, that the soul is the recipient on which He bestows spiritual blessings by contemplation, the knowledge and the love

of Himself together ; that is, He gives it loving knowledge without the instrumentality of its discursive acts,
because it is no longer able to form them as before.

35. At this time, then, the direction of the soul must
be wholly different from what it was at first. If formerly it was supplied with matter for meditation and it
did meditate, now that matter must be withheld and
meditation must cease, because, as I have said, it cannot meditate, do what it will, and distractions are the
result.* If before it looked for fervour and sweetness
and found them, let it look for them no more nor desire
them ; and if it attempt to seek them, not only will it
not find them, but it will meet with aridity, because it
turns away from the peaceful and tranquil good secretly
bestowed upon it, when it attempts to fall back on the
operations of sense. In this way it loses the latter
without gaining the former, because the senses have
ceased to be the channel of spiritual good.

36. Souls in this state are not to be forced to meditate or to apply themselves to discursive reflections
laboriously effected, neither are they to strive after
sweetness and fervour, for if they did so, they would
be thereby hindering the principal agent, Who is God
Himself, for He is now secretly and quietly infusing
wisdom into the soul, together with the loving knowledge

* *Ascent of Mount Carmel*, bk. ii., ch. xiii., and ch. xv. 1.

of Himself, without many divers distinct or separated
acts. But He produces them sometimes in the soul,
and that for some space of time. The soul then must be
lovingly intent upon God without distinctly eliciting
other acts beyond these to which He inclines it ; it must
be as it were passive, making no efforts of its own, purely,
simply, and lovingly intent upon God, as a man who
opens his eyes with loving attention. For as God is
now dealing with the soul in the way of bestowing by
simple and loving knowledge, so the soul also, on its
part, must deal with Him in the way of receiving by
simple and loving knowledge, so that knowledge may
be joined to knowledge, and love to love ; because it
is necessary here that the recipient should be adapted
to the gift, and not otherwise, and that the gift may be
accepted and preserved as it is given.

37. It is evident, therefore, that if the soul does not
now abandon its ordinary way of meditation, it will
receive this gift of God in a scanty and imperfect manner,
not in that perfection with which it is bestowed ; for the
gift being so grand, and an infused gift, cannot be received
in this scanty and imperfect way. Consequently, if the
soul will at this time make efforts of its own, and encourage another disposition than that of passive loving
attention, most submissive and calm, and if it does not
abstain from its previous discursive acts, it will place a

barrier against those graces which God is about to communicate to it in this loving knowledge. He gives His grace to beginners in the exercise of purgation, as I have said,* and afterwards with an increase of the sweetness of love.

38. But if the soul is to be the recipient of His grace passively, in the natural way of God, and not in the supernatural way of the soul, it follows that, in order to be such a recipient, it must be perfectly detached, calm, peaceful, and serene, as God is ; it must be like the atmosphere, which the sun illumines and warms in proportion to its calmness and purity. Thus the soul must be attached to nothing, not even to meditation, not to sensible or spiritual sweetness, because God requires a spirit free and annihilated, for every act of the soul, even of thought, of liking or disliking, will hinder and disturb it, and break that profound silence of sense and spirit necessary for hearing the deep and soft voice of God, Who, in the words of Osee, speaks to the heart in solitude ; † it is in profound peace and tranquillity that the soul, like David, is to listen to God, Who will speak peace unto His people.‡ When this takes place, when the soul feels that it is silent and listens, its loving attention must be most pure, without a thought of self, in a manner self-

---

* *Dark Night*, bk. 1, ch. viii.
† Os. ii. 14.   ‡ Ps. lxxxiv. 9.

forgotten, so that it shall be wholly intent upon hearing, for thus it is that the soul is free and ready for that which our Lord requires at its hands.

39. This tranquillity and self-forgetfulness are ever attended with a certain interior absorption ; and, therefore, under no circumstances whatever, either of time or place, is it lawful for the soul, now that it has begun to enter the state of contemplation, tranquil and simple, to recur to its previous meditation, or to cleave to spiritual sweetness, as I have said, and at great length, in the tenth chapter of the first book of the *Dark Night*, and previously in the last chapter of the second, and in the first of the third book of the *Ascent of Mount Carmel*. It must detach itself from all spiritual sweetness, rise above it in freedom of spirit ; this is what the prophet Habacuc did, for he says of himself, ' I will stand upon my watch ' over my senses—that is, I will leave them below—' and fix my step upon the munition ' of my faculties—that is, they shall not advance a step even in thought—' and I will behold to see what will be said to me,' * that is, I will receive what God shall communicate to me passively.

40. I have already said † that to contemplate is to receive, and it is impossible to receive the highest wisdom, that is contemplation, otherwise than in a silent spirit,

* Habac. ii. 1.   † *Dark Night*, bk. 1, ch. ix.

detached from all sweetness and particular knowledge.
So the Prophet Isaias when he says, ' Whom shall He
teach knowledge ? and whom shall He make to understand the thing heard ? them that are weaned from the
milk,' that is from sweetness and personal likings, ' that
are plucked away from the breasts,' * from reliance on
particular knowledge. Take away, O spiritual man, the
mote and the film from thine eye, and make it clean, and
then the sun will shine for thee, and thou shalt see clearly,
establish thy soul in the freedom of calm peace, withdraw
it from the yoke and slavery of the miserable efforts of
thine own strength, which is the captivity of Egypt—for
all thou canst do is little more than to gather straw for
the bricks—and guide it into the land of promise flowing
with milk and honey.

41. O spiritual director, remember it is for this liberty
and holy rest of sons that God calls the soul into the
wilderness ; there it journeys in festal robes, with ornaments of gold and silver,† for the Egyptians are spoiled
and their riches carried away.‡ Nor is this all : the
enemies of the soul are drowned in the sea of contemplation, where the Egyptian of sense finds no support for his
feet, leaving the child of God free, that is the spirit, to
transcend the narrow limits of its own operations, of its
low views, rude perceptions, and wretched likings. God

* Is. xxviii. 9.　　　　† Exod. xxxiii. 4.　　　　‡ *Ib.* xii. 35.

does all this for the soul that He may give it the sweet manna, which, though ' it contains all that is delicious and the sweetness of every taste ' *—objects of desire for the soul according to thy direction—and though it is so delicious that it melts in the mouth, thy penitent shall not taste of it, if he desires anything else, for he shall not receive it.

42. Strive, therefore, to root out of the soul all desire of consolation, sweetness, and meditations ; do not disquiet it about spiritual things, still less about earthly things ; establish it in perfect detachment, and in the utmost possible solitude. For the greater its progress in this, and the more rapidly it attains to this calm tranquillity, the more abundant will be the infusion of the spirit of divine wisdom, the loving, calm, lonely, peaceful, sweet ravisher of the spirit. The soul will feel itself at times enraptured, gently and tenderly wounded, not knowing by whom, how, or when, because the Spirit communicates Himself to it without effort on its part. The least work of God in the soul in this state of holy rest and solitude is an inestimable good, transcending the very thought of the soul and of its spiritual guide, and though it does not appear so then, it will show itself in due time.

43. What the soul is now conscious of is a certain

* Wisd. xvi. 20.

estrangement and alienation from all things around it, at one time more than at another, with a certain sweet aspiration of love and life of the spirit, an inclination to solitude, and a sense of weariness in the things of this world, for when we taste of the spirit, the flesh becomes insipid. But the interior goods which silent contemplation impresses on the soul without the soul's consciousness of them, are of inestimable value, for they are the most secret and delicious unctions of the Holy Ghost, whereby He secretly fills the soul with the riches of His gifts and graces ; for being God, He doeth the work of God as God.

44. These goods, then, these great riches, these sublime and delicate unctions, this knowledge of the Holy Ghost, which, on account of their exquisite and subtile pureness, neither the soul itself, nor he who directs it, can comprehend, but only He Who infuses them in order to render it more pleasing to Himself—are most easily, even by the slightest application of sense or desire to any particular knowledge or sweetness, disturbed and hindered. This is a serious evil, grievous and lamentable. O how sad and how wonderful ! The evil done is not perceived, and the barrier raised between God and the soul is almost nothing, and yet it is more grievous, an object of deeper sorrow, and inflicts a greater stain, than any other, though seemingly more important, in

common souls which have not attained to such a high state of pureness. It is as if a beautiful painting were roughly handled, besmeared with coarse and vile colours; for the injury done is greater, more observable, and more deplorable, than it would be if a multitude of common paintings were thus bedaubed.

45. Though this evil be so great that it cannot be exaggerated, it is still so common that there is scarcely one spiritual director who does not inflict it upon souls whom God has begun to lead by this way to contemplation. For, whenever God is anointing a soul with the unction of loving knowledge, most delicate, serene, peaceful, lonely, strange to sense and imagination; whenever He withholds all sweetness from it, and suspends its power of meditation—because He reserves it for this lonely unction, inclining it to solitude and quiet —a spiritual director will appear, who, like a rough blacksmith, knows only the use of his hammer, and who, because all his knowledge is limited to the coarser work, will say to it : Come, get rid of this, this is waste of time and idleness : arise and meditate, resume thine interior acts, for it is necessary that thou shouldest make diligent efforts of thine own ; everything else is delusion and folly. Such a director as this does not understand the degrees of prayer, nor the ways of the Spirit, neither does he consider that what he recommends the soul to

do is already done, since it has passed beyond meditation and is detached from the things of sense ; for when
the goal is reached, and the journey ended, all further
travelling must be away from the goal.

46. Such a director, therefore, is one who understands
not that the soul has already attained to the life of the
Spirit, wherein there is no reflection, and where the
senses cease from their work ; where God is Himself
the agent in a special way, and is speaking in secret to
the solitary soul. Directors of this kind bedaub the
soul with the coarse ointments of particular knowledge
and sensible sweetness, to which they bring it back ;
they rob it of its loneliness and recollection, and consequently disfigure the exquisite work which God was
doing within it. The soul that is under such guidance
as this fails in one method and does not profit by the
other.

47. Let spiritual directors of this kind remember,
that the Holy Ghost is the principal agent here, and the
real guide of souls ; that He never ceases to take care
of them and never neglects any means by which they
may profit and draw near unto God as quickly as possible,
and in the best way. Let them remember that they
are not the agents, but instruments only to guide souls
by the rule of the faith and the law of God, according
to the spirit which God gives to every one. Their aim

therefore should be, not to guide souls by a way of their own suitable to themselves, but to ascertain, if they can, the way by which God Himself is guiding them. If they cannot ascertain it, let them leave these souls alone and not disquiet them. Let them adapt their instructions to the direction of God, and endeavour to lead their penitents into greater solitude, liberty, and tranquillity, and not fetter them when God is leading them on.

48. The spiritual director must not be anxious or afflicted because the soul is doing nothing, as he imagines, for provided the soul of his penitent be detached from all particular knowledge, from every desire and inclination of sense ; provided it abide in the self-denial of poverty of spirit, emptied of darkness and sweetness, weaned from the breast—for this is all that the soul should look to, and all that the spiritual director is to consider as within the province of them both—it is impossible—according to the course of the divine goodness and mercy—that God will not perform His own work, yea, more impossible than that the sun should not shine in a clear and cloudless sky. As the sun rising in the morning enters the house if the windows are open, so God, the unsleeping keeper of Irsael,* enters the emptied soul and fills it with good things. God is,

* Ps. cxx. 4.

like the sun, above our souls and ready to enter within them.

49. Let spiritual directors, therefore, be content to prepare souls according to the laws of evangelical perfection, which consists in detachment, and in the emptiness of sense and spirit. Let them not go beyond this with the building, for that is the work of our Lord alone, from Whom cometh ' every perfect gift.' * For, ' unless our Lord build the house, they labour in vain that build it.' † And as He is the supernatural builder, He will build up in every soul, according to His own good pleasure, the supernatural building. Do thou, who art the spiritual director, dispose the natural faculties by annihilating them in their acts—that is thy work ; the work of God, as the Wise Man says,‡ is to direct man's steps towards supernatural goods by ways and means utterly unknown to thee and thy penitent.

50. Say not, therefore, that thy penitent is making no progress, or is doing nothing, for if he have no greater pleasure than he once had in particular knowledge, he is advancing towards that which is above nature. Neither do thou complain that thy penitent has no distinct perceptions, for if he had he would be making no progress, because God is incomprehensible, surpassing all understanding. And so the further the penitent

* St. James i. 17.　　† Ps, cxxvi, 1,　　‡ Prov. xvi. 1, 9.

advances, the further from himself must he go, walking by faith, believing and not seeing ; he thus draws nearer unto God by not understanding, than by understanding. Trouble not thyself about this, for if the understanding goes not backwards occupying itself with distinct knowledge and other matters of this world, it is going forwards ; for to go forwards is to go more and more by faith. The understanding, having neither the knowledge nor the power of comprehending God, advances towards Him by not understanding.* Thus, then, what thou judgest amiss in thy penitent is for his profit : namely, that he does not perplex himself with distinct perceptions, but walks onwards in perfect faith.

51. Or, you will say, perhaps, that the will, if the understanding have no distinct perceptions, will be at the least idle, and without love, because we can love nothing that we do not know. That is true as to the natural actions of the soul, for the will does not love or desire anything of which there is no distinct conception in the understanding. But in the matter of infused contemplation, it is not at all necessary for the soul to have distinct knowledge, or to form many discursive acts, because God Himself is then communicating to it loving knowledge, which is at the same time heat

* St. Teresa, *Life*, ch. xviii. 18.

and light indistinctly, and then according to the state of the understanding love also is in the will. As the knowledge is general and dim—the understanding being unable to conceive distinctly what it understands—so the will also loves generally and indistinctly. For as God is light and love in this delicate communication, He informs equally the understanding and the will, though at times His presence is felt in one more than in the other. At one time the understanding is more filled with knowledge than the will with love, and at another, love is deeper than knowledge.

52. There is no reason, therefore, to be afraid of the will's idleness in this state, for if it ceases to elicit acts directed by particular knowledge, so far as they depend on itself, God inebriates it with infused love through the knowledge which contemplation ministers, as I have just said.

53. These acts of the will which are consequent upon infused contemplation are so much the nobler, the more meritorious and the sweeter, the nobler the source, God, Who infuses this love and kindles it in the soul, for the will is now near unto God, and detached from other joys. Take care, therefore, to empty the will and detach it from all its inclinations, for if it is not going backwards, searching after sweetness and comfort, even though it have none in God distinctly felt, it is really

advancing upwards above all such things to God, seeing
that it is without any particular pleasure.

54. And though the penitent have no particular
comfort in God distinctly apprehended, though he does
not make distinct acts of love, he does find more comfort
in Him in that general secret and dim infusion than if
he were under the influence of distinct acts of knowledge,
because the soul sees clearly then that not one of them
can furnish so much comfort and delight as this calm and
lonely infusion. He loves God, too, more than all lovely
things, because the soul has thrown aside all other joys
and pleasures ; they have become insipid.

55. There is no ground for uneasiness here, for if the
will can find no rest in the joys and satisfactions of
particular acts, there is then real progress, because not
to go backwards, embracing what is sensible, is to go
onwards to the unapproachable, Who is God. Hence,
then, if the will is to advance, it is to do so more by
detachment from, than by attachment to, what is
pleasurable and sweet. Herein is fulfilled the precept of
love, namely, that we are to love Him above all things.
And if this love is to be perfect, we must live in perfect
detachment, and in a special emptiness of all things.

56. Neither are we to be distressed when the memory
is emptied of all forms and figures ; for as God is without form or figure, the memory is safe when emptied of

them, and draws thereby the nearer to God. For the more the memory relies on the imagination, the further it departs from God, and the greater the risks it runs ; because God, being above our thoughts, is not cognisable by the imagination. These spiritual directors, not understanding souls who have already entered into the state of quiet and solitary contemplation, because they know it not, and perhaps have never advanced beyond the ordinary state of reflection and meditation themselves, look upon the penitents, of whom I am speaking, as idle—for ' the sensual man,' the man who still dwells with the feelings of the sensual part of the soul, ' perceiveth not these things that are of the Spirit of God ' *—disturb the peace of that calm and tranquil contemplation given them by God, and force them back to their former meditations.

57. This is followed by great loss, repugnance, dryness, and distractions on the part of penitents, who desire to abide in quiet and peaceful self-recollection. These directors will have them strive after sweetness and fervours, though in truth they should have given them a wholly different advice. The penitents are unable to follow their direction, being incapable of meditating as before ; because the time for that is past, and because that is not their road. They are, therefore, doubly

* I Cor. ii. 14.

disquieted, and imagine themselves in the way of perdition. Their directors encourage them in this supposition, dry up their spirit, rob them of the precious unctions which God gave them in solitude and calm—and this is a great evil—and furnish them with mere mud instead, for they lose the former, and labour in vain with the latter.

58. Such directors as these do not really know what spirituality is. They wrong God most grievously, and treat Him irreverently, putting forth their coarse hands to the work which He is doing Himself. It has cost God not a little to have brought souls thus far, and He greatly prizes this solitude to which He has led them, this emptiness of their faculties, for He has brought them thither that He may speak to their heart,* that is what He always desires. He is now taking them by the hand, and reigning in them in the abundance of peace. He has deprived the discursive faculties of their strength, wherewith they had ' laboured all the night ' and had taken nothing.† He feeds them now in spirit, not by the operation of sense, because the senses together with their acts cannot contain the spirit.

59. How precious in His sight is this calm, or sleep, or annihilation of the senses, His words in the Canticle show : ' I adjure you, O daughters of Jerusalem, by the

* Os. ii. 14.   † St. Luke v. 5.

roes and harts of the fields, that you stir not up nor awake my beloved till she please.' * Those words tell us how much He loves this sleep and lonely oblivion of the soul, by the mention of those solitary and retiring animals. But the spiritual directors of whom I am speaking will not suffer their penitents to rest, they insist upon continual labour, so that God shall find no opportunity for doing His work ; the work of God they undo and disfigure by the work of the soul, and the little foxes that destroy the vines are not driven away. God complains of these directors by the mouth of the Prophet, saying, ' You have devoured the vineyard.' †

60. But it may be said that these directors err, perhaps, with good intentions, because their knowledge is scanty. Be it so ; but they are not therefore justified in giving the rash counsels they do, without previously ascertaining the way and spirit of their penitent. And if they do not understand the matter, it is not for them to interfere in what they do not comprehend, but rather to leave their penitent to others who understand him better than they. It is not a light fault to cause by a wrong direction the loss of inestimable blessings, and to endanger a soul. Thus, he who rashly errs, being under an obligation to give good advice—for so is every one in the office he assumes—shall not go unpunished for the

* Cant. iii. 5.   † Is. iii. 14.

evil he has done. The affairs of God are to be handled with great caution and watchful circumspection, and especially this, which is so delicate, and so high, and where the gain is infinite if the direction given be right, and the loss also infinite if it be wrong.

61. But if you say that such a director may be excused—though for my part I do not see how—you must at least admit that he is inexcusable who keeps a penitent in his power for certain empty reasons and considerations known only to himself: he will not go unpunished. It is quite certain that a soul which is to make progress in the spiritual life, and which God is ever helping, must change its method of prayer, and be in need of a higher direction and of another spirit than those of such a director. Not all directors have the knowledge which every event on the spiritual road requires : neither are they all qualified to determine how a given soul is to be directed under every circumstance of the spiritual life ; at least they must not presume that they are, or that it is God's will that a particular soul shall not advance further. As it is not everyone who can trim a block of wood, can also carve an image out of it ; nor can everyone form the outlines who can carve ; nor can everyone who fashions the outlines paint them, as neither can everyone who can paint perfect and complete the image : for everyone of these can do

only what he understands himself ; and if any one of them were to attempt that which is not within the compass of his skill, he would spoil the statue.

62. So is it in the spiritual life ; for if a director whose only work it is to trim the rude block, that is, to make his penitent despise the world, and mortify his desires ; or if, further, it be that of the carver, who is to guide the soul into holy meditations, and his science extend no further, how can he guide his penitent to the highest perfection of the finished portrait, to that delicate colouring which consists not in the rough hewing of the wood, nor in the carving thereof, nor even in the formation of the outlines, but is rather a work which God Himself perfects in the soul with His own hand ? It is therefore quite certain that such a director as this, whose teaching is ever the same, cannot help driving back the penitent whom he subjects to it, or, at the least, hindering his advancement. For what will be the state of the image, if nothing be done to it but to rough-hew the wood and beat it with a mallet ? What is this, but the discipline of the faculties ? When shall the image be finished ? When shall it be ready for God to colour it ?

63. Is it possible that any spiritual director can think himself qualified for all this ? that he looks upon himself as sufficiently skilful, so as to render the teaching of

7

another needless for his penitent ?   Granting even that
he is qualified for the whole direction of a particular
soul, because, perhaps, such a soul has no vocation for
a higher walk, it is almost impossible that he can be
also a sufficient guide for all whom he hinders from passing out of his hands into the hands of others.   God
leads every soul by a separate path, and you will scarcely
meet with one spirit which agrees with another in one
half of the way by which it advances.   Who can be
like St. Paul, who ' became all things to all men, that
he might save all ? ' *

64. Thou art thus become a tyrant of souls, the
robber of their liberties, claiming for thyself all the
freedom of the evangelical doctrine, and taking care
that none of thy penitents leave thee ; yea, still further,
and much worse, should it come to thy knowledge that
any of them had gone elsewhere for direction, or to discuss a question which it was not convenient to submit
to thee ; or if God had led them for the purpose of
learning what thou teachest not—I say it with shame—
thou art jealous, like a husband of his wife.   This is not
zeal for the honour of God, but the zeal which cometh
out of thine own pride and presumption.   How couldest
thou be sure that thy penitent had no need of other
guidance than thine ?   With such directors God is

* 1 Cor. ix. 22.

angry and he threatens to chastise them, saying : ' Woe to the shepherds of Israel . . . you eat the milk and you clothed yourself with the wool . . . but my flock you did not feed. . . . I will require my flock at their hand.' *

65. These directors, therefore, ought to leave their penitents at liberty, yea, they lie under an obligation to allow them to have recourse to the advice of others, and always to receive them again with a cheerful counte-nance ; for they know not by what way God intends to lead them, especially when their present direction is not suited to them. That, indeed, is a sign that God is leading their penitents by another road, and that they require another director ; they should, therefore, counsel the change, for a contrary course of proceeding springs from a foolish pride and presumption.

66. Let me now pass on from this and speak of other means, fatal as the plague, which these directors, or others worse than they, make use of in the guidance of souls. When God sends into a soul the unctions of holy desires, and leads it to give up the world, draws it on to change its state of life, and to serve Him by despising the world—it is a great matter in His eyes that souls should have advanced to this, for the things of the world are not according to the heart of God—these directors, with their human reasonings and worldly

* Ezech. xxxiv. 2, 10

motives, contrary to the doctrine of Christ, at variance with mortification and contempt of all things, consulting their own interest or pleasure, or fearing where no fear is, interpose delays or suggest difficulties, or, what is worse, take away all such good thoughts from the hearts of their penitents. These directors have an evil spirit, are indevout and exceedingly worldly ; unaccustomed to the ways of Christ, they do not enter in themselves by the strait gate, neither will they suffer others to enter. These are they whom our Lord threatens in the gospel, saying : ' Woe to you lawyers, for you have taken away the key of knowledge : you yourselves have not entered in, and those that were entering you have hindered.' *

67. These directors are in truth like barriers before the gate of heaven, forgetting that God has called them to the functions they exercise that they may compel those to enter in whom He has invited. He has given them this charge in the gospel, but they, on the contrary, compel their penitents not to enter in by the narrow gate which leadeth unto life.† Such a director as this is one of the blind guides who thwarts the direction of the Holy Ghost. This happens in many ways ; some err knowingly ; others ignorantly ; but both the one and the other shall be punished ; for by taking upon

* St. Luke xi. 52.   † St. Matth. vii. 13, 14.

themselves the office which they fill, they are bound to
understand and consider what they do.

68. The other blind guide that disturbs the soul in
this interior recollection is Satan, who, being blind himself, desires to render the soul blind also. He labours,
therefore, when the soul has entered into those deep
solitudes, wherein the delicate unctions of the Holy
Ghost are infused—he hates and envies the soul for this,
because he sees it fly beyond his reach, adorned with the
riches of God—to throw over the soul's detachment and
estrangement from the world, certain cataracts of knowledge, and the darkness of sensible sweetness, sometimes
good, the more to entice the soul, and to draw it back
to the way of sense. He would have it fix its eyes on
this, and make use of it with a view of drawing near to
God, relying upon this kind of knowledge, and sensible
sweetness. By this means Satan distracts the soul, and
easily withdraws it from that solitude and recollection
wherein the Holy Ghost worketh secretly His great
marvels within.

69. And then the soul, naturally prone to sensible
satisfactions and sweetness—especially if it aims at them
—is most easily led to rely upon such knowledge and
sweetness, and so draws back from the solitude wherein
God was working. For as the soul, as it seemed, was
doing nothing then, this new way appears preferable,

because it is something, while solitude seemed to be nothing. How sad it is that the soul, not understanding its own state, should, for one mouthful, disqualify itself for feeding upon God Himself ; for He offers Himself to be its food when He absorbs it in these spiritual and solitary unctions of His mouth.

70. In this way, the evil spirit, for a mere nothing, inflicts upon souls the very greatest injuries, causing the loss of great riches, and dragging them forth, like fish with a trifling bait, out of the depths of the pure waters of the spirit, where they were engulfed and drowned in God, resting upon no created support. He drags them to the bank, and supplies them with objects whereon to rest, and makes them walk on the earth painfully, that they may not float on ' the waters of Siloe, that run with silence,' * bathed in the unctions of God. It is wonderful how much Satan makes of this : and as a slight injury inflicted on the soul in this state is a great one, you will scarcely meet with one which has gone this way that has not suffered great injuries, and incurred grievous losses. Satan stations himself with great cunning on the frontiers between sense and spirit ; there he deludes the soul, and feeds the senses, interposing sensible things to keep it back, and hinder it from escaping out of his hands.

* Is. viii. 6.

71. The soul, too, is most easily taken by these devices, for it knows as yet of nothing better ; neither does it dream that this is a loss, yea, rather, it looks on it as a great gain, and accepts the suggestions of the evil one gladly, for it thinks that God has come to visit it ; consequently it omits to enter into the inner chamber of the Bridegroom, and stands at the door to see what is passing without in the sensual part of itself.

72. The devil, in the words of Job, ' seeth every high thing ' * that relates to souls that he may assail them. If, therefore, a soul becomes recollected, he labours to disturb it by horrors and fears, or by bodily pains, or outward noise and tumults, that he may ruin it ; he strives to draw its attention to the tumult he excites, and to fix it upon what is passing without, and to withdraw it from the interior spirit, but when he fails in his efforts he leaves it alone.   So easily does Satan squander great riches and bring about the ruin of these precious souls, though he thinks this of more consequence than the fall of many others, that he looks upon it as a small matter because of the ease with which he effects it and because of the little trouble it costs him.

73. We may also understand in the same sense the following words spoken by God to Job : † ' Lo ! he shall sop up the river and shall not marvel : and he hath confi-

* Job xli. 25.   † *Ib.* xl. 18, 19.

dence that Jordan '—the highest perfection—' may run into his mouth. In his eyes as with a hook he shall take him, and with stakes he shall bore through his nostrils.' That is, he will turn away the soul from true spirituality by means of the arrows of distinct knowledge wherewith he pierces it, for the breath which goeth out through the nostrils in one volume becomes dispersed if the nostrils be pierced, and escapes through the divers perforations.

74. Again it is said, ' The beams of the sun shall be under him, and he shall strew gold under as dirt.'* He causes souls that have been enlightened to lose the marvellous beams of divine knowledge, takes away and disperses abroad the precious gold of the divine adorning by which souls had been made rich.

75. O souls, now that God shows you mercies so great, leading you into solitude and recollection, withdrawing you from the labours of sense, do not return thereto. If your own exertions were once profitable, enabling you to deny the world and your own selves when you were but beginners, cease from them now when God of His mercy has begun to work in you, for now they will only embarrass you. If you will be careful to lay no stress on your own operations, withdrawing them from all things, and involving them in nothing,— which is your duty in your present state—and wait

* Job xli. 21.

lovingly and sincerely upon God at the same time—
doing no violence to yourselves except to detach yourselves wholly, so as not to disturb your tranquillity and
peace—God Himself will feed you with the heavenly
food, since you cease to hinder Him.

76. The third blind guide of the soul is the soul itself,
which, not understanding its own state, disturbs and
injures itself. For as the soul knows of no operations
except those of sense ; when God leads it into solitude,
where it cannot exert its faculties and elicit the acts it
elicited before, and as it appears to itself then to be doing
nothing, it strives to elicit its previous acts more distinctly and more sensibly. The consequence is distraction, dryness, and disgust in that very soul which
once delighted in the calm peace and spiritual silence,
wherein God Himself was in secret infusing His sweetness. It sometimes happens that God persists in keeping
the soul in this quiet calm, and that the soul persists
in crying out with the imagination, and in walking with
the understanding. Such souls are like children in their
mothers' arms, who, unable to walk, cry, and struggle
with their feet, demanding to be allowed to walk alone,
but who cannot walk themselves, and suffer not their
mothers to do so either. These souls make God resemble
a painter whose work is hindered because the subject
he portrays will not be still.

77. The soul, then, should keep in mind that it is now making greater progress than it could make by any efforts of its own, though it be wholly unconscious of that progress. God Himself is carrying it in His own arms, and thus it happens that it is not aware that it is advancing. Though it thinks that it is doing nothing, yet in truth more is done than if itself were the agent ; for God Himself is working. If this work be invisible, that is nothing strange, for the work of God in the soul is not cognisable by sense, because silently wrought : ' The words of the wise are heard in silence.' * Let the soul abandon itself to the hands of God and trust in Him. He that will do so shall walk securely, for there is no danger then unless the soul should attempt anything in its own strength, or by the wilful exercise of its proper faculties.

78. Let us now return to the deep caverns of the senses, in which I said the sufferings of the soul are ordinarily very great when God is anointing it, and preparing it for union with Himself by His subtile and delicate unctions. These unctions of God are so subtil that, penetrating into the inmost depths of the soul, they so dispose it, and so fill it with sweetness, that the sufferings and fainting of the soul through its great desire in the immense void of the caverns are immeasur-

* Eccles. ix. 17.

able. Now if the unction which disposes the caverns
for the union of the spiritual marriage be so wonderful,
what shall the accomplishment thereof be ? Certain it
is that as the hunger and thirst and suffering of the
caverns, so will be the satisfaction, fulness, and delight
thereof. According to the perfection of these dispositions will be the delight of the fruition and possession
of the sense of the soul, which is the power and energy
of its very substance for perceiving and delighting in
the objects of its faculties.

79. These faculties are with great propriety called
caverns. For as the soul is conscious that they admit
the profound intelligence and splendours of the lamps, it
sees clearly also, that they are deep in proportion to the
depth of the intelligence and love ; that they have space
and capacity commensurate with the distinct sources of
the intelligence, of the sweetness and delight which it
receives in them. All this is received and established
in the cavern of the sense of the soul which is the capacity
thereof for possession, perception, and fruition. Thus,
as the common sense of the imagination is the place
where all the objects of the outward senses are treasured
up, so is this common sense of the soul enlightened and
made rich by a possession so grand and so glorious.

' Dim and dark.'

80. The eye sees not for two reasons ; either because

it is in darkness or is blind. God is the light and the true object of the soul, and when He does not shine upon it, it is then in darkness, though its power of vision may be most perfect. When the soul is in sin, or when it occupies the desires with other things than God, it is then blind. Though the light of God be not wanted to it then, yet, being blind, it cannot see the light because of its blindness, which is the practical ignorance in which it lives. Before God enlightened the soul in its transformation it was in darkness and ignorant of His great goodness, as was the Wise Man before he was enlightened, for he says, ' He enlightened my ignorance.'*

81. Speaking spiritually, it is one thing to be blind and another to be in darkness. Blindness proceeds from sin, but darkness does not necessarily involve sin, and it happens in two ways. There is natural darkness where the light of natural things shines not, and there is supernatural darkness where there is no knowledge of many supernatural things. Here the soul says with regard to them both, that the understanding without God abode in darkness. For until our Lord said, ' Let light be,' † darkness was upon the face of the deep of the cavern of the soul's sense. The deeper the cavern

---

* Ecclus. li. 26. ' Ignorantias meas illuminavit.' This text is no. longer in the Vulgate. See *Dark Night*, bk. ii., ch. xii. 2.

† Genes. i. 3.

when God shines not upon it, the deeper is the darkness thereof. Thus it is impossible for it to lift up the eyes to the divine light, yea the divine light is not even thought of, because never seen or known to exist ; there is therefore no desire for it. And the soul desires darkness rather than light, and so goes on from darkness to darkness, led by darkness, for darkness can lead only to darkness again.

82. David saith, ' day to day uttereth word and night to night showeth knowledge,' * thus as the deep of darkness calleth another deep, and the deep of light another deep of light ; † like calling upon like, so the light of grace which God had before given to the soul, and by which He opened the eyes of it from the deep to behold the divine light, and made it pleasing to Himself, calls to another deep of grace, namely, the divine transformation of the soul in God, wherein the eye of sense is enlightened and rendered pleasing.

83. The eye was also blind in that it took pleasure in other than God. The blindness of the higher and rational sense is caused by the desire which, like a cloud or a cataract, overlies and covers the eye of reason, so that it shall not see what is before it. Thus, then, the grandeur and magnificence of the divine beauty are rendered invisible, so far as the pleasure of sense is

* Ps. xviii. 3.   † *Ib.* xli. 8.

followed. For if we cover the eye with anything, however trifling it may be, that is enough to obstruct the vision of objects before us be they ever so large. Thus, then, a single desire entertained by the soul suffices to hinder the vision of all the divine grandeurs which are higher than its desires and longings. Who can say how impossible it is for the soul, subject to desires, to judge of the things of God ? for he that would judge aright of these must cast away all desires, because he cannot judge aright while subject thereto ; for in that case he will come to consider the things of God not to be God's, and those things which are not God's to be the things of God.

84. While this cloud and cataract cover the eye of the judgment, nothing is visible except the cloud, sometimes of one colour, sometimes of another, according to circumstances, and men will take the cloud for God, because they see nothing beside the cloud which overshadows the sense, and God is not comprehended by sense. Thus, desire and sensual satisfactions hinder the knowledge of high things, as it is written, ' The bewitching of vanity obscureth good things, and the inconstancy of concupiscence perverteth the understanding ' that is without malice.* Those persons, therefore, who are not so spiritual as to be purified from

* Wisd. iv. 12.

their desires and inclinations, but are still sensual, believe those things to be important which are in truth of no account in spirituality, being intimately connected with sense ; they make no account of and despise the deep things of the spirit, which are further removed from sense, yea sometimes they look upon them as folly, as we learn from St. Paul, ' The sensual man perceiveth not these things that are of the Spirit of God : for it is foolishness to him and he cannot understand.' *

85. The sensual man is he who still lives according to the desires and inclinations of nature, and even though these desires come occasionally into contact with the things of the spirit, yet, if man cleaves to spiritual things with his natural desires, they are still natural desires only. The spirituality of the object is little to the purpose, if the desire of it proceed from itself, having its root and strength in nature. What ! you will say, is it not a supernatural desire to desire God ? No, not always ; but only then when the motive is supernatural, and when the strength of the desire proceeds from God ; that is a very different thing. When the desire comes from thyself, so far as it relates to the manner thereof, it is nothing more than natural. So, then, when thou art attached to thy spiritual tastes, exerting thine own natural desire, thou bringest a cataract over thine eye,

* 1 Cor. ii. 14.

thou art sensual, incapable of perceiving or judging what is spiritual, for that transcends all natural sense and desire.

86. If thou still doubtest, I have nothing further to add except to bid thee read over again what I have written, and that done perhaps the doubts will vanish. What I have said is the substance of the truth, and I cannot now enlarge upon it. The sense of the soul hitherto in darkness without the divine light and blinded by its desires, is now such that its deep caverns, because of the divine union, ' with unwonted brightness give light and warmth together to the Beloved.'

' With unwonted brightness give light and
warmth together to the Beloved.'

87. These caverns of the soul's faculties being now in a wonderful way among the marvellous splendours of the lamps which burn within them, being lighted and burning in God, remit back to God in God, in addition to their self-surrender to Him, those very splendours which they receive from Him in loving bliss ; they also, turning to God in God, being themselves lamps burning in the brightness of the divine lamps, return to the Beloved that very light and warmth of love which they receive from Him. Now, indeed, they give back unto Him, in the way they receive them, those very splendours which He communicates, as crystal reflects the rays of

the sun ; but in a nobler manner, because of the inter-
vention of the will.

'With unwonted brightness ; '

88. That is, strange and surpassing all imagination
and description. For the perfection of beauty wherein
the soul restores to God what it has received from Him
is now in conformity with that perfection wherewith the
understanding—made one with that of God—received
the divine wisdom : and the perfection wherewith the
will restores to God in God that very goodness He gave
it—for it was given only to be restored—is in conformity
with that perfection wherein the will is united with
the will of God. In the same way, proportional to the
perfection of its knowledge of God's greatness, united
therewith, does the soul shine and give forth the warmth
of love. And according to the perfection of the other
divine attributes communicated to the soul, such as
strength, beauty, justice, are those perfections wherewith
the spiritual mind, now in enjoyment, gives back to the
Beloved in the Beloved the very light and warmth
which it is receiving from Him.

89. The soul now being one with God is itself God
by participation, and though not so perfectly as it will
be in the world to come, is still, as I have said, as God
in a shadow.* Thus, then, the soul, by reason of its

* See *Spiritual Canticle*, Stanza xxxix. 6, 7.

8

transformation, being a shadow of God, effects through God in God what He effects within it Himself by Himself, because the will of both is one. And as God is giving Himself with a free and gracious will, so the soul also with a will, the more free and the more generous the more it is united with God in God, is, as it were, giving back to God—in that loving complacency with which it regards the divine essence and perfections—God Himself.

90. This is a mystic and affective gift of the soul to God, for then the soul seems in truth to have God for its own possession, and that it possesses Him, as His adopted child, by a right of ownership, by the free gift of Himself made unto it. The soul gives to the Beloved, Who is God Himself, what He had given to it. Herein it pays the whole debt, for the soul giveth as much voluntarily with inestimable joy and delight, giving the Holy Spirit as its own of its own free will, so that God may be loved as He deserves to be.

91. Herein consists the inestimable joy of the soul, for it sees that it offers to God what becomes Him in His Infinite Being. Though it be true that the soul cannot give God to God anew, because He is always Himself in Himself, still it does so, perfectly and wisely, giving all that He has given it in requital of His love; this is to give as it is given, and God is repaid by this gift of the soul; nothing less could repay Him. He

receives this gift of the soul as if it were its own, with
kindness and grace, in the sense I have explained ;
and in that gift He loves it anew, and gives Himself
freely to it, and the soul also loves Him anew. Thus,
there is in fact a mutual interchange of love between
the soul and God in the conformity of the union, and
in the matrimonial surrender, wherein the goods of
both, that is the divine essence, are possessed by both
together, in the voluntary giving up of each to the other.
God and the soul say, the one to the other, what the
Son of God said to the Father, ' All My things are Thine,
and Thine are Mine, and I am glorified in them.'* This
will be verified in the fruition of the next life without
intermission, and is verified in the state of union when
the soul's communion with God energises in an act of love.

92. The soul can offer such a gift, though far greater
than itself, just as he who possesses many kingdoms and
nations as his own, though greater than he, can bestow
them upon whom he will. This is the soul's great
delight, that it sees itself giving unto God more than
itself is worth, that it gives Himself to God so generously,
as if God were its own, in that divine light and warmth
of love which He Himself has given it. This is effected
in the life to come through the light of glory and of
love, and in this life by faith most enlightened and by

* St. John xvii. 10.

love most enkindled. Thus it is that the deep caverns of sense, with unwonted brightness give light and heat together to the Beloved. I say together, because the communication of the Father and of the Son and of the Holy Ghost in the soul is one ; they are the light and the fire of love therein.

93. I must here observe briefly on the perfection of beauty wherewith the soul makes this gift. In the act of union, as the soul enjoys a certain image of fruition, caused by the union of the understanding and will in God, it makes this gift of God to God, and of itself to Him, in most wonderful ways ; delighting itself therein, and constrained thereto. As to love, the soul stands before God in strange beauty, as to the shadow of fruition in the same way, and also as to praise and gratitude.

94. As to the first, which is love, the soul has three grand perfections of beauty. It loves God by means of God. This is an admirable perfection, because, set on fire by the Holy Ghost, and having the Holy Ghost dwelling within it, it loves as the Father loves the Son, as it is written, ' that the love wherewith Thou hast loved Me, may be in them, and I in them.'* The second perfection is that it loves God in God, for in this union the soul is vehemently absorbed in the love of God,

* St. John xvii. 26.

and God communicates Himself with great vehemence to it. The third perfection of beauty is that the soul now loves God for what He is ; for it loves Him not merely because He is bountiful, good, and generous to it, but much more earnestly, because He is all this essentially in Himself.

95. There are also three perfections of beauty in that shadow of fruition, marvellously great. The first is that the soul enjoys God here, united with God Himself, for as the understanding of the soul is one with wisdom and goodness, and perceives so clearly—though not perfectly as in the life to come—it delights greatly in all these, clearly understood, as I said before.* The second perfection of beauty is that the soul delights itself in God alone without the admixture of any created thing. The third is that it enjoys Him alone as He is, without the admixture of any selfish feeling, or of any created object.

96. There are also three principal perfections of beauty in the praise of God which the soul offers to Him in union. The first is that the soul offers it as an act of duty, because it recognises this as the end of its creation ; as it is written, ' This people have I formed for Myself, they shall show forth My praise.'† The second is, that it praises Him for blessings received,

* § 4, *supra*.   † Is. xliii. 21.

and because of the joy it has in praising our Lord Who is so great. The third is, that it praises Him for what He is in Himself, for if the praises of God were unaccompanied by any pleasure at all, still it would praise Him because He is Who He is.

97. Gratitude also has three principal perfections. The first is, thanksgiving for all natural and spiritual blessings, and for all benefits received. The second is the great delight of praising God, in the way of thanksgiving, for the soul is moved with great vehemence in the act. The third is that the soul gives thanks unto God only because He is, which is much more efficacious and more delightful.

STANZA IV

How gently and how lovingly
Thou liest awake in my bosom,
Where Thou secretly dwellest alone ;
And in thy sweet breathing,
Full of grace and glory,
How tenderly Thou fillest me with Thy love.

EXPLANATION

HERE the soul turns towards the Bridegroom in great love, magnifying Him and giving Him thanks for two

marvellous graces which He sometimes effects within
the soul through its union with Himself. The soul, too,
observes on the way He produces them and on their
effects upon itself.

2. The first effect is the awakening of God in the
soul, and that in gentleness and love. The second is the
breathing of God in the soul, and that in grace and bliss
given in that breathing. ' The effect of this upon the soul
is to make it love Him sweetly and tenderly. The
stanza therefore may be paraphrased as follows : O how
gently and how lovingly dost thou lie awake in the
depth and centre of my soul, where Thou in secret and
in silence alone, as its sole Lord, abidest, not only as
in Thine own house or in Thine own chamber, but also
as within my own bosom, in close and intimate union :
O how gently and how lovingly ! Sweet to me is Thy
breathing in that awakening, for it is full of grace and
glory. O with what tenderness dost Thou inspire me
with love of Thee ! The figure is borrowed from one
awaking from sleep, and drawing his breath, for the
soul in this state feels it to be so.

> ' How gently and how lovingly
> Thou liest awake in my bosom.'

3. The awakenings of God in the soul are manifold,
and so many that were I to describe them I should never
end. This awakening, to which the soul refers here, the

work of the Son of God, is, in my opinion, of the highest
kind, and the source of the greatest good to the soul.
This awakening is a movement of the Word in the depth
of the soul of such grandeur, authority and glory, and of
such profound sweetness, that all the balsams, all the
aromatic herbs and flowers of the world seem to be
mingled and shaken together for the production of that
sweetness : that all the kingdoms and dominions of
the world, all the powers and virtues of heaven are
moved ; this is not the whole, all the virtues, substance,
perfections and graces of all created things, shine forth
and make the same movement in unison together.   For
as St. John saith, ' What was made in Him was life,'*
and in Him moves and lives ; as the Apostle says, ' In
Him we live and move and are.' †

4. The reason is this : when the grand Emperor
would reveal Himself to the soul, moving Himself in the
light He gives, and yet not moving in it—He, upon
whose shoulder is the principality,‡ that is, the three
worlds of heaven, earth, and hell, and all that is in them,
and Who sustains all by the word of His power §—then
all seem to move together.   As when the earth moves,
all natural things upon it move with it ; so is it when the

---

* St. John i. 3.   The Carmelite Breviary used by St. John of the
Cross till 1586 maintains the old punctuation : " Without Him was
made nothing.   What was made in Him was life."

† Acts xvii. 28.   ‡ Is. ix. 6.   § Heb. i. 3.

Prince moves, for He carries his court, not the court Him. This, however, is an exceedingly imperfect illustration ; for here not only all seem to move, but also to manifest their being, their beauty, power, and loveliness, the root of their duration and, life in Him. There, indeed, the soul sees how all creatures, higher and lower, live, continue, and energise in Him, and understands the words of the Wise Man, ' by me kings reign . . . by me princes rule, and the mighty decree justice.' *

5. Though it is true that the soul here sees that all these things are distinct from God, in that they have a created existence ; it understands them in Him with their force, origin and strength, it knows also that God in His own essence is, in an infinitely pre-eminent way, all these things, so that it understands them better in Him, their First Cause, than in themselves. This is the great joy of this awakening, namely, to know creatures in God, and not God in His creatures : this is to know effects in their cause, and not cause by its effects.

6. This movement in the soul is wonderful, for God Himself moves not. Without movement on the part of God, the soul is renewed and moved by Him ; the divine life and being and the harmony of creation are revealed with marvellous newness, the cause assuming the designation of the effect resulting from it. If we regard

* Prov. viii. 15.

the effect, we may say with the Wise Man that God moves,
' for wisdom is more moveable than all moveable things,'
not because it moves itself but because it is the source
and principle of all motion, and ' permanently in herself,
she reneweth all things ; ' * this is the meaning of the
words, ' more moveable than all moveable things.'

7. Thus, then, strictly speaking, in this movement
it is the soul that is moved and awakened, and the expression ' awake ' is correct. God however being always,
as the soul sees Him, the mover, the ruler, and the giver
of life, power, graces, and gifts to all creatures, contains
all in Himself, virtually, actually, and supremely. The
soul beholds what God is in Himself, and what He is
in creatures. So may we see, when the palace is thrown
open, in one glance, both the magnificence of him who
inhabits it, and what he is doing. This, according to
my understanding of it, is this awakening and vision
of the soul ; it is as if God drew back some of the many
veils and coverings that are before it, so that it might
see what He is ; then indeed—but still dimly, because
all the veils are not drawn back, that of faith remaining
—the divine face full of grace bursts through and shines,
which, as it moves all things by its power, appears
together with the effect it produces, and this is the
awakening of the soul.

* Wisd. vii. 24.

8. Though all that is good in man comes from God, and though man of himself can do nothing that is good, it may be said in truth, that our awakening is the awakening of God, and our rising the rising of God. 'Arise, why sleepest Thou, O Lord?'* saith the Psalmist. That is in effect to say, Raise us up and awake us, for we are fallen and asleep. Thus then, because the soul had fallen asleep, and could never rouse itself again, and because it is God alone who can open its eyes, and effect its awakening, this awakening is most properly referred to God : ' Thou awakest in my bosom.'

' Thou awakest in my bosom.'

9. Awake us, O Lord, and enlighten us, that we may know and love the good things which Thou hast set always before us, and we shall know that Thou art moved to do us good, and hast had us in remembrance. It is utterly impossible to describe what the soul, in this awakening, knows and feels of the majesty of God, in the inmost depths of its being, that is, its bosom. For in the soul resounds an infinite power, with the voice of a multitude of perfections, of thousands and thousands of virtues, wherein itself abiding and subsisting, becomes ' terrible as an army set in array,' † sweet and gracious in Him who comprehends in Himself all the sweetness, and all the graces of His creation.

* Ps. xliii. 23.   † Cant. vi. 3.

10. But here comes the question, how can the soul bear so vehement a communication while in the flesh, when in truth it has not strength for it without fainting away ? The mere sight of Assuerus on his throne, in his royal robe, glittering with gold and precious stones, was so terrible in the eyes of Esther, that she fainted through fear, so awful was his face. ' I saw Thee, my lord, as an angel of God, and my heart was troubled, for fear of thy glory.' * Glory oppresses him who beholds it, if it does not glorify him. How much more then is the soul now liable to faint away, when it beholds not an angel but God Himself, the Lord of the angels, with His face full of the beauty of all creatures, of terrible power and glory, and the voice of the multitude of His perfections. It is to this that Job referred when he said, ' We have heard scarce a little drop of His word ; who shall be able to behold the thunder of His great-ness ? ' † and again, ' I will not that He contend with me with much strength, nor that He oppress me with the weight of His greatness.' ‡

11. The soul, however, does not faint away and tremble at this awakening so powerful and glorious. There are two reasons for this : one is that it is now in the state of perfection, and therefore the lower portion of it is purified and conformed to the spirit, exempt from

* Esth. xv. 16.   † Job. xxvi. 14.   ‡ *Ib*. xxiii. 6.

that pain and loss which spiritual communications involve, when the sense and spirit are not purified and disposed for the reception of them. 2. The second and the principal reason is that referred to in the first line of this stanza, namely, that God shows Himself gentle and loving. For as He shows His greatness and glory to the soul in order to comfort and exalt it, so does He favour and strengthen it also, and sustain its natural powers while manifesting His greatness gently and lovingly. This is easy enough to Him, Who with His right hand protected Moses that he might behold His glory.*

12. Thus the soul feels God's love and gentleness to be commensurate with His power, authority, and greatness, for in Him these are all one. Its delight is therefore vehement, and the protection it receives strong in gentleness and love, so that itself being made strong may be able without fainting away to sustain this vehement joy. Esther, indeed, fainted away, but that was because the king seemed unfavourable towards her, for with ' burning eyes ' he ' showed the wrath of his breast,'† but the moment he looked graciously upon her, touched her with his sceptre and kissed her, she recovered herself, for he had said to her, ' I am thy brother, fear not.'

13. So is it with the soul in the presence of the King

* Exod. xxxiii. 22. † Esth. xv. 10.

of kings, for the moment He shows Himself as its Bridegroom and Brother, all fear vanishes away. Because in showing unto it, in gentleness and not in anger, the strength of His power and the love of His goodness, He communicates to it the strength and love of His breast, ' leaping from His throne ' * to caress it, as the bridegroom from his secret chamber, touching it with the sceptre of His majesty, and as a brother embracing it. There the royal robes and the fragrance thereof, which are the marvellous attributes of God ; there the splendour of gold which is charity, and the glittering of the precious stones of supernatural knowledge ; and there the face of the Word full of grace, strike the queenly soul, so that, transformed in the virtues of the King of heaven, it beholds itself a queen : with the Psalmist, therefore, may it be said of it, and with truth, ' The queen stood on Thy right hand in gilded clothing, surrounded with variety.' † And as all this passes in the very depths of the soul, it is added immediately, ' Where Thou secretly dwellest alone.'

' Where Thou secretly dwellest alone.'

14. He is said to dwell secretly in the soul's bosom, because, as I have said,‡ this sweet embracing takes place in the inmost substance and powers of the soul. We must keep in mind that God dwells in a secret and

* Esth. xv. 11, 12.   † Ps. xliv. 10.   ‡ Stanza i. 9 ; ii. 9.

hidden way in all souls, in their very substance, for if He did not, they could not exist at all. This dwelling of God is very different in different souls ; in some He dwells alone, in others not ; in some He dwells contented, in others displeased ; in some as in His own house, giving His orders, and ruling it ; in others, as a stranger in a house not His own, where He is not permitted to command, or to do anything at all. Where personal desires and self-will least abound, there is He most alone, most contented, there He dwells as in His own house, ruling and directing it, and the more secretly He dwells, the more He is alone.

15. So then in that soul wherein no desire dwells, and out of which all images and forms of created things have been cast, the Beloved dwells most secretly Himself, and the purer the soul and the greater its estrangement from everything but God, the more intimate His converse and the closer His embrace. He dwells there then in secret, for Satan cannot come near His dwelling place, nor see the embracing ; nor can any understanding explain it. But He is not hidden from the soul in the state of perfection, for such a soul is ever conscious of His presence. Only in these awakenings He seems to awake Who before was asleep in the soul's bosom ; and though it felt and enjoyed His presence, He seemed as one sleeping within.

16. O how blessed is that soul which is ever conscious of God reposing and resting within it. How necessary it is for such a soul to flee from the matters of this world, to live in great tranquillity, so that nothing whatever shall disturb the Beloved ' at His repose.' *

17. He is there as it were asleep in the embraces of the soul, and the soul is, in general, conscious of His presence, and, in general, delights exceedingly in it. If He were always awake in the soul, the communications of knowledge and love would be unceasing, and that would be a state of glory. If He awakes but once, merely opening His eyes, and affects the soul so profoundly, what would become of it if He were continually awake within it ?

18. He dwells secretly in other souls, those which have not attained to this state of union, not indeed displeased, though they are not yet perfectly disposed for union : these souls in general are not conscious of His presence, but only during the time of these sweet awakenings, which however are not of the same kind with those already described, neither indeed are they to be compared with them. But the state of these souls is not so secret from the devil, nor so far above the reach of the understanding as the other, because the

* Cant. i. 11.

senses always furnish some indications of it by the excitement into which they are thrown. The senses are not perfectly annihilated before the union is complete, and they manifest their power in some degree, because they are not yet wholly spiritual. But in this awakening of the Bridegroom in the perfect soul, all is perfect because He effects it all Himself in the way I have spoken of. In this awakening, as of one aroused from sleep and drawing breath, the soul feels the breathing of God, and therefore it says : ' In Thy sweet breathing.'

' And in Thy sweet breathing, full of grace and glory,
    how tenderly Thou fillest me with Thy love.'

19. I would not speak of this breathing of God, neither do I wish to do so, because I am certain that I cannot ; and indeed were I to speak of it, it would seem then to be something less than what it is in reality. This breathing of God is in the soul, in which in the awakening of the deep knowledge of the Divinity, He breathes the Holy Ghost according to the measure of that knowledge which absorbs it most profoundly, which inspires it most tenderly with love according to what it saw. This breathing is full of grace and glory, and therefore the Holy Ghost fills the soul with goodness and glory, whereby He inspires it with the love of Himself, transcending all glory and all understanding. This is the reason why I say nothing more.

9

INSTRUCTIONS AND PRECAUTIONS

INSTRUCTIONS AND PRECAUTIONS

TO BE CONTINUALLY OBSERVED BY HIM WHO
SEEKS TO BE A TRUE RELIGIOUS AND TO
ARRIVE QUICKLY AT GREAT PERFECTION

IF any religious desires to attain in a short time to holy recollection, spiritual silence, detachment and poverty of spirit—where the peaceful rest of the spirit is enjoyed, and union with God attained ; if he desires to be delivered from all the hindrances which created things put in his way, to be defended against all the wiles and illusions of Satan, and to be protected against himself, he must strictly practise the following instructions.

If he will do this, with ordinary attention, without other efforts or other practices, at the same time carefully observing the obligations of his state, he will advance rapidly to great perfection, acquire all virtue and attain unto holy peace.

All the evils to which the soul is subject proceed from the three enemies already mentioned : the world, the devil, and the flesh. If we can hide ourselves from these we shall have no combats to fight. The world is less difficult, and the devil more difficult, to understand ; but the flesh is the most obstinate of all, and the last to be overcome together with the ' old man.' If we do not conquer the three, we shall never perfectly conquer one ; and if we conquer one, we shall also conquer the others in the same proportion.

In order to escape perfectly from the evils which the world inflicts, there are three things to be observed.

FIRST PRECAUTION

The first is, preserve an equal love and an equal forgetfulness of all men whether relatives or not ; withdraw your affections from the former as well as from the latter, yea even rather more from the former, on account of the ties of blood, for the natural affection which men feel for their kindred always subsists. You must mortify this affection if you are to attain unto spiritual perfection. Look upon your kindred as strangers, and you will thereby the more completely discharge your duty to them ; for by not withdrawing your heart from God on their account, you will fulfil your duties towards them better by not giving to them those affections which are due unto God.

Do not love one man more than another, for if you do you will fall into error. He whom God loves most is the most worthy of love, and you do not know who he is. But if you strive to forget all men alike—as holy recollection requires you to do—you will escape all error, whether great or small. Do not think about them ; have nothing to say to them either good or bad. Avoid them as much as you possibly can. If you do not observe this, as things go, you never will become a good religious, you will never attain to holy recollection, nor will you get rid of your imperfections. If you will indulge yourself here, Satan will in some way or other delude you, or you will delude yourself under the pretence of good or evil.

If you will observe this direction you will be safe ; and in no other way can you get rid of the imperfections and escape the evils which result to your soul from intercourse with men.

SECOND PRECAUTION

The second precaution against the world relates to temporal goods. If you desire in earnest to escape the evils which worldly goods occasion, and restrain your excessive desires, you must hold all personal possession in abhorrence, and cast from you every thought about it. You must not be solicitous about what you eat or drink or wear, or about any created thing whatever :

you must not be 'solicitous for to-morrow,' but occupy
yourself with higher things—with the kingdom of God,
that is, fidelity unto Him—for all these things, as our
Lord says in the gospel, 'shall be added unto you.' *
He who takes care of the beasts of the field will not forget you. If you do this you will attain unto silence,
and have peace in your senses.

THIRD PRECAUTION

The third precaution is most necessary, that you may
avoid all evil in your relation with the other religious of
the community. Many persons from not heeding this
have not only lost their peace of mind, but have fallen,
and fall daily, into great disorders and sin. Be especially
careful never to let your mind dwell upon, still less your
tongue to speak of, what is passing in the community,
its past or present state. Do not speak of any religious
in particular, do not discuss his condition or his conversation, or his actions, however grave, either under
the cloak of zeal, or of remedying what seems amiss,
except only to him who of right should be spoken to,
and then at the fitting time. Never be scandalised or
surprised at what you see or hear, and preserve yourself in complete forgetfulness of all. If you lived among
the angels and gave heed to what was going on many

* St. Matth. vi. 33.

things would seem to you not to be good, because you do not understand them.

Take warning from the example of Lot's wife who, because she was disturbed at the destruction of Sodom, turned back to behold it. God punished her for this, and she 'was turned into a pillar of salt.' * This teaches you that it is the will of God, even if you were living among devils, you should so live as not to turn back in thought to consider what they are doing, but forget them utterly. You are to keep your soul wholly for God, and not to suffer the thought of this or that to disturb you.

Be sure of this, there is no lack of stumbling blocks in religious houses, because there is no lack of devils who are labouring to throw down the saints. God permits this in order to try them and to prove them, and if you be not on your guard, you will never become a religious, do what you may, neither will you attain to holy detachment and recollection, or avoid loss. If you live otherwise, in spite of your zeal and good intentions, Satan will lay hold of you in one way or another, and indeed you are already sufficiently in his power, when your soul is allowed such distractions as these. Remember those words of the apostle St. James, ' If any man think himself to be religious, not bridling his

* Genes. xix. 26.

tongue, this man's religion is vain.' * This is applicable to the interior, quite as much as to the exterior, tongue—to thoughts as well as words.

THREE PRECAUTIONS NECESSARY TO BE OBSERVED IN ORDER TO BE DELIVERED FROM THE DEVIL IN RELIGION

If you wish to escape from Satan in religion, you must give heed to three things, without which you cannot be in safety from his cunning. In the first place I would have you take this general advice, which you should never forget, namely, that it is the ordinary practice of Satan to deceive those who are going on unto perfection by an appearance of good : he does not tempt them by what seems to be evil. He knows that they will scarcely regard that which they know to be wrong. You must therefore continually distrust that which seems to be good, and especially when obedience does not intervene. The remedy here is the direction of one whom you ought to consult. Let this then be the

FIRST PRECAUTION

Never set about anything, however good and charitable it may seem, either to yourself or to any other,

* St. Jam. i. 26.

whether in the community or out of it, except under obedience, unless you are bound to do it by the rule of your order. If you do this you will acquire merit, and be in security. You will be safe against yourself and against evil ; you will also avoid evils of which you are ignorant, and of which God will require an account one day. If you do not observe this in little things as well as in great, notwithstanding your apparent progress, Satan will most certainly deceive you little or much. Even if your whole error consist in your not being guided in everything by obedience, you are plainly wrong, because God wills obedience rather than sacrifice,* and the actions of a religious are not his own, but those of obedience, and if he withdraws them from the control of obedience, he will have to give account of them as lost.

SECOND PRECAUTION

The second precaution is a very necessary one, because the devil interferes exceedingly in the matter to which it refers. The observance of it will bring great gain and profit, and the neglect great loss and ruin. Never look upon your superior, be he who he may, otherwise than if you were looking upon God, because he stands

* I Kings xv. 22.

in His place. Keep a careful watch over yourself in this matter, and do not reflect upon the character, ways, or conversation, or habits of your superior. If you do, you will injure yourself, and you will change your obedience from divine into human, and you will be influenced by what you see in your superior, and not by the invisible God Whom you should obey in him. Your obedience will be in vain, or the more barren the more you are troubled by the untowardness, or the more you are pleased by the favour, of your superior. I tell you that a great many religious in the way of perfection are ruined by not looking upon their superiors as they ought ; their obedience is almost worthless in the eyes of God, because influenced by human considerations. Unless you force yourself therefore to be indifferent as to who your superior may be, so far as your private feelings go, you will never be spiritual, neither will you faithfully observe your vows.

THIRD PRECAUTION

The third precaution against Satan is this : strive with all your heart after humility in thought, word, and deed, taking more pleasure in others than in yourself, giving way in every thing to others, and doing so as far as you can from a sincere heart. In this way you will overcome evil with good, drive the devil away, and have joy in your heart. Deal thus with those who are less agreeable to you ; for be assured, if you do not, you will never have true charity nor make progress in it. Be always more ready to receive instruction from any one than to give it, even to the least of your brethren.

THREE PRECAUTIONS TO BE OBSERVED BY THOSE WHO WOULD CONQUER THEMSELVES, AND MASTER THE CUNNING OF THE FLESH

FIRST PRECAUTION

If you wish to be delivered from the uneasiness and imperfections of which the habits and conversation of the religious may be the occasion, and profit by everything that may happen, you must keep in mind that you entered the community to be mortified and tried, and that all those in authority in it are there, as in truth they are, for that purpose. Some have to mortify you by words, others by deeds, and others by what they think of you ; in all this you are to submit yourself, unresisting as a statue to the polisher, the painter, and the gilder of it. If you do not, you will never be able to live as you ought with the religious in the monastery ; you will not attain to holy peace, nor will you escape from much evil.

SECOND PRECAUTION

Never omit any practices, if they are such as befit you, because they are disagreeable ; neither observe them because they are pleasant, unless they be as necessary as those which are not agreeable. Otherwise you will find it impossible to acquire firmness, and conquer your weakness.

THIRD PRECAUTION

In all your spiritual exercises never set your eyes upon the sweetness of them and cling to it, but rather on that in them which is unpleasant and troublesome, and accept it. If you do, you will never destroy self-love, nor acquire the love of God.

LETTERS

LETTERS

LETTER I

TO MOTHER CATHERINE OF JESUS, BAREFOOTED CARMEL-
ITE AND COMPANION OF ST. TERESA OF JESUS *

JESUS

Be in your soul, my daughter Catherine. Although I
know not where you are, I write you these few lines,
trusting that our Mother will forward them to you if you
are not with her. And even if you are not with her,
comfort yourself with me, who am further away and
alone here. For since I was swallowed by that whale,†
and cast forth upon this distant shore, I have not been
counted worthy to see her or the saints who are down
there. God has done it for our good ; for loneliness is a
file, and to suffer darkness is the way to great light.

God grant that we may not walk in darkness. Oh !

---

* This nun was professed at Valladolid, December 13, 1572. St.
Teresa, who esteemed her highly, took her to Palencia, and afterwards
to Burgos, nominating her sub-prioress. She died at Soria, date
not on record.

† The prison of the Monastery of Toledo.

how many things would I fain say to you ! But I am
writing very much in the dark, fearing that you may
not receive this letter ; and therefore I break off without finishing it. Recommend me to God. I will say
no more from here, for I am weary.

Your servant in Christ,

FR. JOHN OF THE CROSS.

From BAEZA : the 6th of July, 1581.

LETTER II *

TO THE RELIGIOUS IN VEAS.

JESUS be in your souls : My daughters are thinking
that I have lost sight of them because I do not write,
and that I have ceased to consider how easily they can
become saints and rejoice in the Bridegroom Whom they
love with great gladness and in strong security. I will
come to Veas, and you will see that I have not forgotten
you. We shall then see the treasures obtained by pure
love and on the pathways of everlasting life ; the
blessed progress you have made in Christ, Whose joy
and crown are His brides. This crown ought not to be

---

* This letter appeared for the first time, copied from the original
kept in the monastery of Pastrana, in the *Life of the Saint*, by Don
Manuel Nuñoz Garnica, Canon of Jaén (Jaén, 1875, p. 411).

rotting on the ground, but rather borne by the hands of the seraphim, and placed with respect and reverence on the head of our Lord.

When the heart is grovelling meanly on the ground the crown rolls in the dust, and is trampled on in every act of meanness. But when man shall ' come to a heart that is high,' according to the words of David,* then shall God be exalted with the crown of the heart of His bride ; wherewith they crown Him in the day of the joy of His coronation, for His delight is to be with the children of men.†

The sources of the waters of interior joy are not on the earth ; the mouth of desire must be opened heavenwards, utterly empty ; and in order that the mouth of desire may be neither closed nor vitiated by the taste of anything, it should be kept perfectly empty and open before Him Who says, ' dilate thy mouth and I will fill it.' ‡ For so it is, he who seeks' for satisfaction in anything is not keeping himself in a state of emptiness that God may fill him with this unspeakable joy ; his hands are encumbered, and he cannot lay hold of that which God is giving him ; as he went to God, so he returned. God save us from these miserable embarrassments by which a freedom so sweet and so delightful is disturbed. Serve God, my daughters beloved in

* Ps. lxiii. 7.   † Prov. viii. 31.   ‡ Ps. lxxx. 11.

Christ, following Him on the road of mortification in all patience and in all silence, with all your soul bent on suffering, having made yourselves executioners of your own will. Mortify yourselves, and if there be anything still living that hinders the interior resurrection of the spirit let it die in your souls. Amen.

Your servant,

FR. JOHN OF THE CROSS.

From MALAGA: November 18, 1586.

LETTER III

TO THE RELIGIOUS OF VEAS

He gives them some spiritual advice, full of heavenly instruction, and worthy of perpetual remembrance

JESUS, MARY

Be in your souls, my daughters in Christ.

Your letter greatly consoled me, and may our Lord reward you for it. It was not from want of will that I have refrained from writing to you, for truly do I wish you all good ; but because it seemed to me that enough had been said already to effect all that was needful, and that what is wanting, if indeed anything be wanting, is

not writing or speaking—whereof ordinarily there is
more than enough—but silence and work. For whereas
speaking distracts, silence and action collect the thoughts,
and strengthen the spirit. As soon therefore as a person understands what has been said to him for his good,
he has no further need to hear or to discuss ; but to
set himself in earnest to practise what he has learnt
with silence and attention, in humility, charity, and
contempt of self ; not turning aside incessantly to seek
after novelties which serve only to satisfy the desire in
outward things—failing however to satisfy it really—
and to leave it weak and empty, devoid of interior virtue.
The result is unprofitable in every way ; for a man
who, before he has digested his last meal, takes another
—the natural heat being wasted upon both—cannot
convert all this food into the substance of his body, and
sickness follows. It is most necessary, my daughters,
to know how to avoid the devil and our own sensuality,
for if we do not we shall find ourselves to be very unprofitable servants, very far away from the virtues of
Christ ; and in the end we shall awake from our sleep
to find our toil and labour to have been the reverse of
what they were. The lamp which we believed to be
alight will be found extinguished, because the breath
whereby we thought to kindle it, served perhaps to put
it out. There are no means to avoid this, and pre-

serve spirituality, better than suffering, doing good works, silence, custody of the senses, the practice of, and the inclination to solitude, forgetfulness of creatures, and of all that is going on, even if the world were to come to an end. Never fail, whatever may befall you be it good or evil, to keep your heart quiet and calm in the tenderness of love, that it may suffer in all circumstances. For so momentous a thing is perfection, and so priceless is spiritual joy, and may God grant that this may be enough ; for it is impossible to make progress but by the way of good works and suffering courageously, always in silence. I have heard, my daughters, *that the soul which is ready to talk and converse with creatures, is not very ready to converse with God ; for if it were, it would be at once drawn forcibly inwards, be silent and avoid all conversation ; for God would that the soul should delight in Him rather than in any creature, however excellent and profitable it may be.* I commend myself to your charitable prayers ; and do you rest assured that, scant as my charity is, it is so bound up in you that I never forget those to whom I owe so much in our Lord. May He be with us all. Amen.

FR. JOHN OF THE CROSS.

From GRANADA : the 22nd of Nov., 1587.

LETTER IV

TO MOTHER ELEANORA BAPTIST, PRIORESS OF THE CONVENT OF VEAS *

The blessed father consoles her under an affliction

JESUS

Be in your soul. Think not, my daughter in Christ, that I am not sorry for you in your troubles, and for those who share them with you ; but when I remember that God has called you to an apostolic life, which is a life of contempt, I am comforted, for He is leading you on that road. God will have a religious to be a religious, that he shall be dead to all things, and all things dead to him ; because He will be his riches, his consolation, his glory, and his bliss. God has conferred a great grace upon your reverence, for now, forgetting all things, you may rejoice in Him alone, caring nothing,

* Eleanora Bautista de Jesús (Perez de Castillejo y Bermudez), born at Alcarraz, entered the convent of Veas, where she made her profession, January 6, 1578. She assisted Ven. Anne of Jesus in the foundation of the convent of Granada, and afterwards became prioress of Veas, and later on of Valencia, where she excelled in the art of training nuns in the religious life. She did not go to Madrid, but died at Valencia in 1604.

in your love of God, for what may come upon you, since
you are no longer your own, but His. Let me know
whether your departure for Madrid is certain, and
whether the mother prioress is coming. I commend
myself especially to my daughters Magdalene and Ana
and to all the rest, not having leisure to write to them.

FR. JOHN OF THE CROSS.

From GRANADA : the 8th of February, 1588.

LETTER V

TO MOTHER ANNE OF ST. ALBERT, PRIORESS OF THE
BAREFOOTED CARMELITES OF CARAVACA *

*He makes known to her by a prophetical inspiration the state of her
soul, and delivers her from scruples*

JESUS

Be in your soul. How long, my daughter, must you
be carried in the arms of others ? I long to see in you
a great detachment of spirit, and such a freedom from

* Anne of St. Albert (de Salcedo), born at Malagon, was one of the
first nuns of that convent, having made her profession in 1569. She
accompanied St. Teresa to Seville, being chosen for the foundation
of Caravaca, which was to be made from there. She died in 1624.

any dependence upon creatures, that all the powers of hell may be unable to disturb you. What useless tears have you been shedding in these last days : How much precious time, think you, have these scruples caused you to throw away ? If you would communicate your troubles to me, go strait to that spotless mirror of the Eternal Father, His only Begotten Son ; for there do I daily behold your soul, and without doubt you will come away consoled, and have no more need to beg at the door of poor people.

Your servant in Christ,

FR. JOHN OF THE CROSS.

From GRANADA.

LETTER VI

TO THE SAME RELIGIOUS

On the same subject

JESUS

Be in your soul, very dear daughter in Christ. Though you say nothing to me, I will say something to you ; let those vain fears which make the spirit cowardly find no place in your soul. Leave to our Lord that which He has given and daily gives ; you seem to measure God by

the measure of your own capacity ; but that must not be
so. Prepare yourself to receive a great grace.

Your servant in Christ,

FR. JOHN OF THE CROSS.

From GRANADA.

LETTER VII

TO THE SAME RELIGIOUS

*The holy father informs her of the foundation of the monastery at Cordova,
and of the removal of the nuns in Seville*

JESUS

Be in your soul. I wrote to you in haste when I left
Granada for the foundation at Cordova. I have since
received your letter there, and those of the gentlemen
who went to Madrid, thinking that they should find me
at the council. You must know, however, that it never
met, for we have been waiting to finish these visitations
and foundations, while our Lord is now making such
haste in the matter, that we are without strength to
follow Him. The friars have been received at Cordova
with the greatest joy and solemnity on the part of the
whole city. No Order has been better received there.
All the clergy and confraternities of Cordova assembled
on the occasion, and there was a solemn procession of

the Most Holy Sacrament from the Cathedral Church—
all the streets being decorated—with great concourse of
people, as on the feast of Corpus Christi.

This took place on the Sunday after Ascension day,
and the bishop preached, praising us much in his sermon.
The house is in the best part of the city, and belongs to
the Cathedral. I am now busied at Seville with the
removal of our nuns, who have bought some very con-
siderable houses; though they cost about 14,000 ducats,
they are worth more than 20,000. They are now
established there. My lord Cardinal is to place the
Blessed Sacrament there with great solemnity on the
feast of St. Barnabas. Before my departure I intend
to establish another house of friars here, so that there
will be two of our Order in Seville. Before the feast of
St. John I shall set forth for Ecija, where, with the
divine blessing, we shall found another ; thence to
Malaga, and then to the council. I wish I had authority
to make this foundation, as I had for the others. I do
not expect much from what is going on ; but I trust
in God that the foundation will be made, and in the
council I will do what I can ; and you may say so to
these gentlemen to whom I am writing.

Send me the little book of the *Stanzas of the Bride*
which I think Sister ——* of the Mother of God will by

* Probably Anne of the Mother of God.

this time have copied. Remember me very specially to señor Gonzalo Muñoz, I do not write for fear of being troublesome to him, and because your reverence will make known to him that which I have here related to you,

> Dearest daughter in Christ,
>> Your servant,
>>> FR. JOHN OF THE CROSS.

From SEVILLE : June, 1586.

LETTER VIII

TO F. AMBROSE MARIANO OF ST. BENEDICT, PRIOR OF MADRID *

Containing wholesome instructions for the training of novices

JESUS

Be in the soul of your reverence. Our need of religious is very great, as your reverence knows, because of the many foundations. It is therefore necessary that your reverence should have patience until father Michael leave this place to wait at Pastrana for the father provincial ;

---

* St. Teresa speaks of this remarkable man in *Foundations*, ch. xvii. 6, *seqq.* After her death he was commissioned to found a convent of friars at Lisbon (1582), and later on at Madrid (1586), where he died in 1594.

the foundation of the convent of Molina being nearly completed. It has seemed good to the fathers also to assign to your reverence a sub-prior, and have made choice of father Angelus, believing that he will agree perfectly with the prior, which is most necessary in a monastery. Your reverence will give to each of these his letters patent, and will not fail to take care that no priest meddle or converse with the novices, for as your reverence knows, nothing is more injurious to them than to pass through many hands, or that strangers should frequent the novices. Since, however, you have so many under your care, it is reasonable that you should help and relieve father Angelus. Give him authority, as he is already sub-prior, that he may be more considered in the house.

It does not seem that father Michael is so much needed here, and he might do greater service to the order elsewhere. Of father Gratian * nothing new, except that father Antony † is now here.

FR. JOHN OF THE CROSS.

From SEGOVIA : Nov. 9, 1588.

[St. John was now the president of the consultors in the absence of Father Nicholas Doria, and therefore wrote this letter as a member of the council.]

* Fr. Jerome Gratian, the friend both of St. Teresa and St. John of the Cross.

† Fr. Antonio de Heredia (Antony of Jesus), with St. John the founder of the order of Discalced friars.

LETTER IX

TO A YOUNG LADY AT MADRID, WHO DESIRED TO BECOME A
BAREFOOTED CARMELITE, AND WHO WAS AFTERWARDS
PROFESSED IN A CONVENT AT ARENAS, IN NEW CASTILE,
AFTERWARDS TRANSFERRED TO GUADALAJARA

JESUS

Be in your soul. Your messenger came at a time when
I was unable to reply before he left the place, and now,
on his return, he is waiting for my letter. May God
ever grant you, my daughter, His holy grace, that
always and in all things you may be wholly occupied
with His holy love ; for to this are you bound, and for
this only He created and redeemed you. On the three
questions there is much to say, more than time and a
letter will allow. I will speak of three other points
which may be profitable to you.

As to sins, God so hates them that He submitted to
die ; it is expedient, in order utterly to root them out,
and never to commit any, to have as little intercourse
with people as possible, avoiding them, and never speaking an unnecessary word on any subject—for all conversation, beyond what necessity or reason absolutely
requires, has never done good to any man, however holy
—and at the same time keeping the law of God with
great exactness and love.

As to the Passion of our Lord, chastise your body with discretion, hate and mortify yourself, and never in anything follow your own will and your own inclination, for that was the cause of His death and passion. Whatever you may do, do it all under the advice of your director. As to the third, which is glory ; in order to meditate well upon it, and love it, you must hold all the riches of the world and all its pleasures to be mere dross, and vanity, and weariness, as, in truth, they are ; and make no account of anything, however great and precious it may be, but only to be well with God ; because the best things here below, when compared with the eternal good for which God created us, are vile and bitter ; and though the bitterness and deformity be but for a moment, they shall abide for ever in the soul which esteems them.

I have not forgotten your matter ; but at present, much as I desire it, nothing can be done. Recommend it earnestly to our Lord, and take our Lady and St. Joseph as your advocates with Him.

Remember me especially to your mother, to whom, as well as to yourself, this letter is addressed ; and do you both pray for me, and ask your friends in their charity to do the same. May God give you His Spirit.

FR. JOHN OF THE CROSS.

From SEGOVIA : February, 1589.

LETTER X

TO A SPIRITUAL SON IN RELIGION, TEACHING HIM HOW
TO EMPLOY HIS WHOLE WILL IN GOD, WITHDRAWING
IT FROM PLEASURE AND JOY IN CREATED THINGS

THE peace of JESUS CHRIST, my son, be ever in your
soul.

I have received the letter of your reverence, wherein
you tell me of the great desire you have, given you by
our Lord, to occupy your will with Him alone, loving
Him above all things, and wherein you also ask me for
some directions how to obtain your end. I rejoice that
God has given you such holy desires, and I shall rejoice
the more at their fulfilment. Remember, then, that all
pleasure, joy, and affections come into the soul through
the will and the desire of those things which seem good,
befitting, and pleasurable, because they seem to be
pleasing and precious ; now the affections of the will
are drawn to them, and the will hopes for them, delights in them when it possesses them, and dreads the
loss of them. The soul, therefore, by reason of these
affections and joys, is disturbed and disquieted.

In order then to annihilate and mortify the desire of
sensible pleasure in things that are not God, your reverence will observe, that everything in which the will

can have a distinct joy is sweet and delectable, because
pleasant in its eyes ; but there is no delectable thing in
which it can have joy and delight in God, for God is not
cognisable by the apprehensions of the other faculties,
and therefore not by the pleasure and desires of the will.
In this life, as the soul cannot taste of God essentially,
so all the sweetness and delight of which it is capable,
and, however great they may be, cannot be God, for
whatever the will takes pleasure in and desires as a
distinct thing, it desires so far as it knows it to be that
which it longs for. For as the will has never tasted of
God, nor ever known Him under any apprehension of
the desire, and therefore comprehends Him not, so by
its taste it can never know Him ; its very being, desire,
and taste can never desire God, because He is above and
beyond all its powers.

It is, therefore, plain that no distinct object whatever
that pleases the will can be God ; and for that reason,
if it is to be united with Him, it must empty itself, cast
away every disorderly affection of the desire, every
satisfaction it may distinctly have, high and low, temporal
and spiritual, so that, purified and cleansed from all
unruly satisfactions, joys, and desires, it may be wholly
occupied, with all its affections, in loving God. For
if the will can in any way comprehend God and be
united with Him, it cannot be through any capacity of

II

the desire, but only by love ; and as all delight, sweetness, and joy, of which the will is sensible, is not love, it follows that none of these pleasing impressions can be the adequate means of uniting the will to God ; the means are an act of the will. And because an act of the will is quite distinct from feeling ; it is by an act that the will is united with God, and rests in Him ; that act is love. This union is never wrought by feeling, or exertions of the desire, for these remain in the soul as aims and ends. It is only as motives of love that feelings can be of service, if the will is bent on going onwards, and for nothing else.

These sweet impressions of themselves do not lead the soul to God, but rather cause it to rest upon them : by an act of the will, that is, by loving God, the soul puts its whole affection, joy, delight, contentment, and love in Him only, casting everything else aside, and loving Him above all things.

For this reason, then, if any one is moved to love God by that sweetness he feels, he casts that sweetness away from Him, and fixes his love upon God, Whom he does not feel ; but if he allowed himself to rest in that sweetness and delight which he feels, dwelling upon them with satisfaction, that would be to love the creature, and that which is of it, and to make the motive an end, and the act of the will would be vitiated ; for as God is incomprehensible and unapproachable, the will, in order to direct its act of love unto God, must not direct it to that which is tangible and capable of being reached by the desire, but must direct it to that which it cannot comprehend nor reach thereby. In this way the will loves that which is certain and true, according to the spirit of the faith, in emptiness and darkness as to its own feelings, above all that it can understand by the operations of the understanding ; its faith and love transcend all that it can comprehend.

He, then, is very unwise, who, when sweetness and spiritual delight fail him, thinks for that reason that God has abandoned him, and when he finds them again, rejoices and is glad, thinking that he has in that way come to possess God.

More unwise still is he who goes about seeking for sweetness in God, rejoices in it, and dwells upon it ; for in so doing, he is not seeking after God with the will grounded in the emptiness of faith and charity, but only in spiritual sweetness and delight, which is a created thing, following herein his own will and fond pleasure. Such an one does not love God purely above all things, which is to direct the whole strength of the will to Him— for by clinging to and resting on the creature by desire, the will does not ascend upwards beyond it to God Who is unapproachable. It is impossible for the will to attain to the sweetness and delight of the divine union, to feel the sweet and loving embraces of God, otherwise than in detachment, in refusing to the desire every pleasure in the things of heaven and earth, for that is the meaning of David, when he said : ' Open thy mouth wide, and I will fill it.' * Now, in this place ' the mouth ' of the will is the desire : the mouth opens, when not filled or hindered with the morsels of its own satisfactions : for when the desire is bent upon anything, it is then restrained, because out of God everything is a restraint.

The soul, then, that is to advance straightway unto God, and to be united with Him, must keep the mouth of the will open, but only for God Himself, in detachment from every morsel of desire, in order that God may fill it with His own love and sweetness : it must hunger and thirst after God alone, seeking its satisfaction in nothing else, seeing that in this life it cannot taste Him as He is. That which may be tasted here, if there be a desire for it, hinders the taste of God.

This is what the prophet Isaias teaches when he says : ' All you that thirst come to the waters.' † He bids all who thirst for God only to come to the fulness of the divine waters of union with Him : namely, those who have not the money of desire. It is most expedient then, for your reverence, if you wish to have great peace in

* Ps. lxxx. 11. † Is. lv. 1.

your soul and to reach perfection, to give up your whole will to God, that it may be united to Him, and utterly detached from the mean and vile occupations of earth. May His Majesty make you as spiritual and as holy as I desire.

FR. JOHN OF THE CROSS.

SEGOVIA, April 14, 1589.

LETTER XI

TO MOTHER ELEONOR OF ST. GABRIEL, A BAREFOOTED
CARMELITE OF SEVILLE *

The holy father and the council command her to accept the office of sub-prioress in the newly founded convent at Cordova

JESUS

Be in your soul, my daughter in Christ. Your letter was very welcome to me, and I thank God that He has been pleased to make use of you in this foundation, which His Majesty has made for your greater profit ; for

. * Born at Ciudad Real, Eleonor de San Gabriel (Mena) made profession at Malagon, June 10, 1571. St. Teresa took her to Seville and made her infirmarian ; later on she became sub-prioress, which office was also entrusted to her in the newly founded convent at Cordova. She had a great desire to accompany the nuns who were chosen for the foundation of a convent at Paris, but in this she was not successful, for she was called back to Seville, where she died, date unknown.

the more He gives, the more does He enlarge our desires, till He leaves us empty that He may fill us with blessings. You shall be well repaid for those which, for the love of your sisters, you forgo in Seville ; for the immense benefits of God can only be received and contained by empty and solitary hearts ; and, therefore, our Lord will have you to be alone, and He really wills it, for He desires to be your only companion. Your reverence must therefore apply your mind to Him alone, and in Him alone content yourself, that in Him you may find all consolation, for if the soul were in heaven, but the will without love, that soul would be still unsatisfied. So also though God be ever with us, if our heart be attached to other things and not fixed on Him alone.

I well believe that those in Seville will be very lonely without your reverence. But, perhaps, you have already done all the good there which you were intended to do, and God wills that you should now work here, for this is one of our principal foundations. To this end, I pray your reverence to afford all the assistance you can to the mother prioress, with great love and union of heart in all things. I know that I need not say this to you, for you have been so long in the order and so experienced that you know all that is usually done in these foundations. For this reason, we chose your reverence. There are religious enough here, but not fitted for this work. Be pleased to remember me particularly to sister Mary of the Visitation, and to sister Juana of St. Gabriel, to whom I return thanks for her letter. May God give your reverence His Holy Spirit.

FR. JOHN OF THE CROSS.

From SEGOVIA: the 8th of July, 1589.

LETTER XII

TO MOTHER MARY OF JESUS, PRIORESS OF THE BARE-FOOTED CARMELITES OF CORDOVA *

Containing useful lessons for religious engaged in the foundation of a new convent, of which they are to be the first stones

JESUS

Be in your soul. You are bound to correspond to the grace of our Lord in proportion to the welcome which you have received, the tidings of which have rejoiced my heart. It was His will that you should enter so poor a dwelling, under the heat of such a burning sun, that you might give edification, and manifest your profession, which is the imitation of Christ in detachment,

* Maria de Jesús (de Sandoval), a nun of Veas, professed in 1576, intimately befriended with St. John of the Cross, sub-prioress at Malaga (1585), foundress and first prioress of Cordova (1589), where she died on August 10, 1604.

in order that those who come to you hereafter may learn in what spirit they must come. I send you all necessary faculties. Be very careful whom you receive at first, because such will be those who follow ; and strive to preserve the spirit of poverty and contempt of all earthly things, being content with God alone : otherwise be assured that you will fall into a thousand temporal and spiritual necessities, you will never, and can never, experience greater necessities than those to which you voluntarily subject your heart : for the poor in spirit is more content and joyful when in want ; having made very nothingness his all, and having found therein fulness and freedom in all things.

O blessed nothingness, and blessed hiddenness of heart, which is of such surpassing virtue as to render all things subject to the soul that will have nothing subject to itself, and casting away all care to burn more and more intensely with love !

Salute all the sisters in our Lord. Tell them that as our Lord has chosen them for the first stones of this building, they must consider well what they ought to be, for upon them, as on a strong foundation, those who follow after them are to be built. Let them profit by the first fruits of the spirit which God gives in the beginning to make a new start on the way of perfection, in all humility and detachment, inward and outward, not

in a childish mind, but with a strong will in mortification and penance. Let them see that Christ costs them
something, and not be like those who seek their own
ease, and look for consolation either in God or out of
Him. But let them suffer either in Him or out of Him,
by silence, hope, and loving remembrance. Make this
known to Gabriela and the sisters at Malaga. To the
others I have already written. The grace of God be
with you. Amen.

FR. JOHN OF THE CROSS.

From SEGOVIA : the 28th of July, 1589.

LETTER XIII

TO MOTHER MAGDALEN OF THE HOLY GHOST, A RELI-
GIOUS OF THE SAME CONVENT OF CORDOVA *

JESUS

Be in your soul, my daughter in Christ. The good
resolutions expressed in your letter make me glad. I
bless God, who provides for all things ! for they will be
greatly needed in the beginnings of foundations that
you may bear poverty, straitness, heat, and labours of

* Magdalen of the Holy Ghost (Rodriguez y Alarcon), a nun of
Veas, who had made her profession August 16, 1577, was chosen for the
foundation of Cordova, where she died in advanced age. See *Spiritual
Canticle*, Introd. p. xvi.

all kinds, in such a manner that none may perceive whether or not all these things are grievous to you. Consider that for such beginnings God will not have delicate and feeble souls, far less such as are lovers of themselves ; and to this end His Majesty helps us more in our beginnings, that they, with moderate diligence, may advance in all virtues. It is assuredly a great grace, and a sign of the divine favour, that, passing by others, He has led you hither. And though the abandonment may have been painful, it is nothing ; for you must in any case have shortly left it all. In order to have God in all things, we must have nothing at all ; for how can the heart, given to one, be given at all to another ?

I say this also to sister Juana, and beg you to pray to God for me. May He be in your heart. Amen.

FR. JOHN OF THE CROSS.

From SEGOVIA : the 28th of July, 1589.

LETTER XIV

TO DOÑA JUANA DE PEDRAÇA, A PENITENT OF THE HOLY FATHER IN GRANADA

JESUS

Be in your soul. I give Him thanks that He has given me the grace not to forget the poor, and not to take my ease, as you say. It would pain me much if I thought you believe what you say. It would be an evil return after so much kindness, when I deserve none. All that is wanting now is that I should forget you ; but consider how that is to be forgotten which is ever present to the soul. But as you are now in the darkness and emptiness of spiritual poverty, you think that all things and all men are failing you ; nor is this wonderful, since you think God Himself fails you. But nothing fails you, nor have you need of any counsel, there is no reason why you should, you will learn nothing, you will find none, for all is groundless suspicion. He who desires nothing but God does not walk in darkness, however blind and poor he may think himself to be ; and he who indulges in no presumptuous thoughts, nor seeks his own satisfaction either in God or in creatures, who does not serve his own will in anything, is in no danger of falling, or in any need of counsel.

You are in the right path, my daughter ; be resigned, and be glad. What ! are you to undertake to guide yourself ? You would do it well, no doubt. You have never been in a better state than now, for you have never been so humble, so submissive ; you have never held yourself, and the things of the world, in greater contempt ; you have never seen yourself to be so bad, nor God to be so good ; you have never served Him so purely and disinterestedly as now. You are not running after the imperfections of your own will, seeking self, as perhaps you once did. What do you mean? What manner of life and conversation do you propose to yourself in this world? In what do you imagine the service of God to consist, except in abstaining from evil, keeping His commandments, and doing His work as well as we can. When you do this, what need have you to seek here and there for other instructions, other lights, other consolations, in which ordinarily lurk many snares and dangers to the soul, which is deceived and deluded by its appetites and perceptions: its very faculties lead it astray.

It is a great grace of God when He so darkens and impoverishes the soul that the senses cannot deceive it. And that it may not go astray, it has nothing to do but to walk in the beaten path of the law of God and of the Church, living solely by faith, dim and true, in certain hope and perfect charity, looking for all its blessings in heaven; living here as pilgrims, beggars, exiles, orphans, desolate, possessing nothing, and looking for everything above.

Rejoice, then, and put your trust in God, Who has given you these tokens; you CAN do so; nay, you ought to do so. If not, you must not be surprised if He should be angry when He finds you so dull, seeing that He has placed you in so safe a path, and led you to so secure a haven. Desire nothing but this, and bend your soul to it, which is in a good and safe condition, and go to communion as usual. Go to confession when you have some definite matter, and speak of that only. When you have anything to say to me write, and that promptly and frequently, which you can always do through doña Ana, if not through the nuns.

I have been somewhat unwell, but am now much better. Fr. John Evangelist,* however, is still suffering. Recommend him to God, and me also, my daughter in our Lord.

FR. JOHN OF THE CROSS.

From SEGOVIA : Oct. 12th, 1589.

LETTER XV

TO MOTHER MARY OF JESUS, PRIORESS OF CORDOVA †

Containing much profitable advice to those whose office is to govern and provide for a community

JESUS

Be in your soul. My daughter in Christ, the cause of my not having written to you for so long a time has been

---

* Fr. John Evangelist, formerly procurator of Granada during St. John's priorship.

† See note to Letter XII.

rather the remote position of Segovia than any want of
will. For my good will has ever been, and I trust in
God shall ever be, the same towards you. I feel for
you in all your trials. But I would not have you take
too much thought concerning the temporal provision for
your house, lest God should forget it ; and you should
fall into great temporal and spiritual distress ; for it is
our over-anxious solicitude which brings us to want.
Cast all your care, my daughter, upon God, and He will
nourish you : for He Who has given and will give the
greater, will not fail to give the less.

Take care that the desire to be in want and poor never
fails you, for that instant your courage will fail, and
your virtues will become weak. For if in time past you
have desired poverty, now that you are in authority you
should desire it still more, and love it ; for the house
must be ruled, and furnished with virtues and heavenly
desires, rather than by carefulness and arrangements
for temporal and earthly things : inasmuch as our Lord
hath bidden us to take no thought for our food, nor for
our raiment, nor for to-morrow. What you have to do
is to train your own soul and the souls of your nuns in
all perfection in religion, in union with God, and rejoicing
in Him alone ; and I will assure you of the rest. It
seems to me very difficult to imagine that the other
houses will come to your help, when you are settled in

so good a position, and have such excellent nuns.   Nevertheless, if I have an opportunity, I will not fail to do
what I can for you.

I wish much consolation to the mother sub-prioress,
and I trust in our Lord that He will give it, and
strengthen her to bear her pilgrimage and exile cheer-
fully for love of Him.   I am writing to her.

Many salutations in our Sovereign Good, to my
daughters Magdalen of St. Gabriel, Mary of St. Paul,*
Mary of the Visitation, and Mary of St. Francis.

May He be ever with your spirit, my daughter.   Amen.

FR. JOHN OF THE CROSS.

From MADRID : the 20th of June, 1590.

LETTER XVI

TO MOTHER ANNE OF JESUS, A BAREFOOTED CARMELITE

OF THE CONVENT OF SEGOVIA †

He consoles her on his not having been chosen superior

JESUS

Be in your soul.   I thank you very much for your letter
and I am more your debtor than I was before.   Though

---

* Nun of Caravaca, professed in 1579, afterwards sent to the foundation of Malaga, and, in 1589, to that of Cordova, where she twice filled
the office of prioress.

† Ana de Jimena, foundress of the convent of Segovia, where she took
the habit and made her profession, July 2, 1575 ; being later on elected
prioress.   She died in 1609, at the age of eighty.

things have not come to pass as you desired, you ought to be glad and give thanks to God ; His Majesty has so ordained, and it is best for all. It remains only that we submit our will, that we may see it in its true light. For when things befall us that we do not like, they seem to us evil and contrary, be they never so good and profitable to our souls. But in this case there is plainly no evil either to me or to any other. To me, indeed, it is most favourable ; for being free and without the care of souls, I may, by God's help, if I like, enjoy peace and solitude, and the blessed fruit of forgetfulness of self and of all created things.*

And others, also, will be the better by my being set aside ; for so will they escape the faults which by reason of my unfittingness they would have committed. What I beg of you, then, my daughter, is to pray to God that He will continue to me this grace ; for I fear that they will send me to Segovia,† and that I shall not be perfectly free. However, I shall do my utmost to escape from this burthen also ; but if I fail, mother Anne of Jesus will not get out of my hands as she expects, and so will not die of grief at losing the opportunity, as she

---

* The Saint refers here to the chapter held in the previous month, in which he was ' set aside,' being elected to no office and deprived of that of provincial of Mexico. See *Life of St. John of the Cross*, by David Lewis, p. 251.

† See *Life, l.c.* p. 253.

thinks, of becoming a very great saint. But whether I go or stay, wherever or however I may be, I will never forget her nor withdraw from the charge of her soul, of which she speaks, because I really desire her eternal good. Now, therefore, until God gives it in heaven, let her exercise herself continually in the virtues of patience and mortification, endeavouring to become like in some measure, through suffering, to our great God, Who was humbled and crucified for us, because our life here is not good if we do not imitate Him. May His Majesty preserve you and make you increase daily in His love, as His holy and well-beloved child. Amen.

FR. JOHN OF THE CROSS.

From MADRID : the 6th July, 1591.

LETTER XVII

TO MOTHER MARY OF THE INCARNATION, PRIORESS OF THE SAME CONVENT *

On the same subject as the preceding

JESUS

Be in your soul. Trouble not yourself, my daughter,

---

* The daughter of Doña Ana de Jimena (see Letter XVI.), Doña Maria de Bracamonte took the habit and made her profession together with her mother. She filled the office of prioress at Segovia at the same time as St. John of the Cross was prior of the friars of that town, and twice at Medina del Campo. She died at Segovia July 29, 1623.

12

about what concerns me, since it troubles me not. The only thing which grieves me much is to see the blame laid upon those to whom it does not belong ; for these things are done not by men, but God, Who knows what is best for us, and orders all things for our good. Think of this only, that all is ordained by God. And do you love where there is no love, and you shall have love. May His Majesty preserve you, and make you grow in His love. Amen.

FR. JOHN OF THE CROSS.

From MADRID : the 6th of July, 1591.

LETTER XVIII

TO DOÑA ANA DE PEÑALOSA *

He informs her of his recent illness

JESUS

Be in your soul, my daughter. I have received here in Peñuela the letter brought me by your servant, and I

* Doña Ana de Mercado y Peñalosa, widow, since 1579, of Don Juan de Guevara, had been instrumental in bringing the Teresian nuns to Granada. She was many years under the direction of St. John of the Cross, who wrote at her request the explanation of the *Living Flame of Love.*

prize exceedingly the kindness thus shown to me. I am going to-morrow to Ubeda, for the cure of a feverish attack, which, having hung about me for more than a week past, makes me think I require medical treatment. It is my desire, however, to return here immediately, as I find great good in this holy solitude. As to the advice you give me not to go with F. Antony, be assured that in this, as in all other matters of the kind, I will be careful. I rejoice greatly to hear that Don Luis * is now a priest of God ; may he be so for many a year, and may His Majesty fulfil all the desires of his soul. Oh, what a blessed state for casting away all solicitude, and speedily enriching his soul ! Congratulate him from me. I dare not venture to ask him to remember me, some day, in the mass, though I, as in duty bound, shall always remember him ; for never shall I, how forgetful soever I be, fail to recollect him, closely bound as he is with the sister whom I ever bear in my memory. I salute my daughter Doña Inez very heartily in our Lord ; and I beg both brother and sister to pray God for me, that He will be pleased to prepare me and take me to Himself.

* Don Luis de Mercado, brother of Doña Ana to whom the letter is addressed, was a native of Segovia, and became auditor of the chancery of Granada, and later on member of the Supreme Council of Castille. He was a great benefactor of the Carmelite friars and nuns of Granada.

Now I remember nothing further that I have to write
to you, and besides, the fever will not suffer me to add
any more. But for this, gladly would I write at much
greater length.

FR. JOHN OF THE CROSS.

From PEÑUELA : Sept. 21, 1591.

CENSURE AND JUDGMENT OF THE BLESSED FATHER ON
THE SPIRIT AND METHOD OF PRAYER OF ONE OF THE
NUNS OF HIS ORDER

IN the kind of effective prayer practised by this soul,
there seem to be five defects, so that I cannot consider
her spirit to be good.   The first is, that she has a great
fondness for her own way : and a true spirit practises
great detachment from all desire.   The second is, that
she is too confident, and has too little fear of delusions ;
the spirit of God is never without fear, in order, as the
Wise Man saith, to keep a soul from sin.*   The third is,
that she wishes to persuade people into the belief that
she is in a good and high state : this is not the fruit
of a true spirit : for that, on the contrary, would wish
to be lightly esteemed, and despised, and does despise
itself.   The fourth and the chief is, that the fruits of

* Prov. xv. 27.

humility are not visible which, when the graces—as she says here—are real, are ordinarily never communicated to the soul without first undoing and annihilating it in an interior abasement of humility. Now, if they had wrought this effect in her, she could not fail to say something, or rather a good deal, about it ; because the first subjects that would suggest themselves to her to speak about, and make much of, are the fruits of humility ; and these in their operations are so effectual, that it is impossible to dissemble them. Though they are not equally observable in all the dealings of God, yet these, which she calls Union, are never found without them. Because a soul is humbled before it is exalted ; * and ' it is good for me that Thou hast humbled me.' † The fifth is, that the style and language she uses do not seem to me those of the spirit she refers to ; for that spirit teaches a style which is more simple, free from affectation, and exaggeration : and such is not the one before me. All this that she says : God spoke to me : I spoke to God : seems nonsense.

What I would say is this : she should not be required nor permitted to write anything on these matters : and her confessor should not seem to hear of them willingly, except to disparage and set aside what she has to say. Let her superiors try her in the practice of virtue only,

* Prov. xviii. 12.　　　　　† Ps. cxviii. 71.

particularly in that of contempt of self, humility, and obedience ; and then at the sound of this blow will come forth that gentleness of soul in which graces so great have been wrought. These tests must be sharp, for there is no evil spirit that will not suffer a good deal for his own credit.

SPIRITUAL MAXIMS

SPIRITUAL MAXIMS

SELECTED FROM THE WRITINGS OF ST. JOHN OF THE CROSS

PROLOGUE

O MY GOD, sweetness and joy of my heart, behold how my soul for love of Thee will occupy itself with these maxims of love and light. For though the words thereof are mine, I have not the meaning and the power, and these are more pleasing to Thee than the language and the knowledge thereof. Nevertheless, O Lord, it may be that some may be drawn by them to serve and love Thee, and profit where I fail : that will be a consolation to me, if through me Thou shalt find in others what Thou canst not find in me. O my Lord, Thou lovest discretion, and light, but love, more than all the other operations of the soul ; so then let these maxims furnish discretion to the wayfarer, enlighten him by the way, and supply him with motives of love for his journey. Away, then, with the rhetoric of the world, sounding words and the dry eloquence of human wisdom, weak and delusive, never pleasing unto Thee. Let us speak

185

to the heart words flowing with sweetness and love, and
such as Thou delightest in.   Thou wilt be pleased herein,
O my God, and it may be that Thou wilt also remove
the hindrance and the stones of stumbling from before
many souls who fall through ignorance, and who for
want of light wander out of the right way, though they
think they are walking in it, and following in all things
in the footsteps of Thy most sweet Son Jesus Christ our
Lord, and imitating Him in their life, state, and virtues
according to the rule of detachment and poverty of spirit.
But, O Father of mercy, do Thou give us this grace, for
without Thee, O Lord, we shall do nothing.

IMITATION OF CHRIST

1.   There is no progress but in the following of Christ,
Who is the way, the truth, and the life, and the Gate by
which he who will be saved must enter.   Every spirit,
therefore, that will walk in sweetness at its ease, shun-
ning the following of Christ, is, in my opinion, nothing
worth.

2.   Your first care must be to be anxiously and lovingly earnest in your endeavours to imitate Christ in
all your actions ; doing every one of them to the utter-

most of your power, as our Lord Himself would have done them.

3. Every satisfaction offered to the senses which is not for God's honour and glory you must renounce and reject for the love of Jesus Christ, Who while upon earth, had, and sought for, no other pleasure than doing the will of His Father; this, He said, was His meat and drink.

4. In none of your actions whatever should you take any man, however holy he may be, for your example, because Satan is sure to put his imperfections forward so as to attract your attention. Rather imitate Jesus Christ, Who is supremely perfect and supremely holy. So doing you will never go astray.

5. Inwardly and outwardly live always crucified with Christ, and you will attain unto peace and contentment of spirit, and in your patience you shall possess your soul.

6. Let Christ crucified alone be enough for you; with Him suffer, with Him take your rest, never rest nor suffer without Him; striving with all your might to rid yourself of all selfish affections and inclinations and annihilation of self.

7. He who makes any account of himself, neither denies himself nor follows Christ.

8. Love tribulations more than all good things, and

do not imagine that you are doing anything when you endure them ; so shall you please Him Who did not hesitate to die for you.

9. If you wish to attain to the possession of Christ, never seek Him without the cross.

10. He who seeks not the cross of Christ, seeks not the glory of Christ.

11. Desire to make yourself in suffering somewhat like our great God, humiliated and crucified ; for life, if not an imitation of His, is worth nothing.

12. What does he know who does not know how to suffer for Christ ? The greater and the heavier the sufferings, the better is his lot who suffers.

13. All men desire to enter into the treasures and consolations of God ; but few desire to enter into tribulations and sorrows for the Son of God.

14. Jesus Christ is but little known of those who consider themselves His friends ; for we see them seeking in Him their own comfort, and not His bitter sorrows.

THE THEOLOGICAL VIRTUES

15. Because it is the function of the theological virtues to withdraw the soul from all that is less than God, it is theirs, therefore, to unite with Him.

16. Without walking truly in the practice of these three virtues, it is impossible to attain to the perfect love of God.

FAITH

17. The way of faith is sound and safe, and along this souls must journey on from virtue to virtue, shutting their eyes against every object of sense and of clear and particular perception.

18. When the inspirations are from God they are always in the order of the motives of His law, and of the faith, in the perfection of which the soul should ever draw nearer and nearer to God.

19. The soul that travels in the light and verities of the faith is secured against error, for error proceeds ordinarily from our own proper desires, tastes, reflections, and understanding, wherein there is generally too much or too little ; and hence the inclination to that which is not seemly.

20. By the faith the soul travels protected against the devil, its strongest and craftiest foe ; and St. Peter knew of no stronger defence against him when he said : ' Resist him, strong in the faith.'

21. The soul that would draw near unto God and

unite itself with Him, must do so by not comprehending rather than by comprehending, in utter forgetfulness of created things ; because it must change the mutable and comprehensible for the immutable and the incomprehensible, Who is God.

22. Outward light enables us to see that we may not fall ; it is otherwise in the things of God, for there it is better not to see, and the soul is in greater security.

23. It being certain that in this life we know God better by what He is not than by what He is, it is necessary, if we are to draw near unto Him, that the soul must deny, to the uttermost, all that may be denied of its apprehensions, both natural and supernatural.

24. All apprehension and knowledge of supernatural things cannot help us to love God so much as the least act of living faith and hope made in detachment from all things.

25. As in natural generation no new form results without the corruption of the one previously existing— for this hinders the former by reason of the contrariety between them—so while the soul is under the dominion of the sensual and animal spirit, the pure and heavenly spirit can never enter.

26. Let no created thing have a place in your heart if you would have the face of God pure and clear in your soul ; yea, rather empty your spirit of all created things,

and you will walk in the divine light ; for God resembles no created thing.

27. The greatest shelter of the soul is Faith ; for the Holy Ghost gives it light : the more pure and refined the soul in a perfect living faith, the greater the infusion of charity, and the greater the communication of supernatural gifts and light.

28. One of the greatest gifts of God to the soul in this life—not permanent but transient—is that deep sense and understanding of God by which it feels and understands clearly, that it can neither understand nor feel Him at all.

29. The soul that leans upon its own understanding, sense, or feeling of its own—all this being very little and very unlike to God—in order to travel on the right road, is most easily led astray or hindered, because it is not perfectly blind in faith, which is its true guide.

30. There is one thing in our day that ought to make us afraid : persons who have hardly begun to make their meditations, if they seem to hear anything in a brief recollection, pronounce it to have come from God ; and so imagine, saying, God has spoken or I have had an answer from God, and it is not so : these persons have been speaking to themselves, out of a longing for such communications.

31. He who should now inquire of God by vision or

revelation would offend Him, because he does not fix his eyes upon Christ alone. To such an one the answer of God is : This is my beloved Son, in Whom I am well pleased, hear Him, and do not seek for new instructions, for in Him I have spoken and revealed all that may be desired and asked for ; I have given Him to be your brother, master, companion, ransom, and reward.

32. We must be guided in all things by the teaching of Christ and His Church, and thereby seek the remedy for our spiritual ignorances and infirmities : it is thus that we shall obtain abundant relief ; and all that goes beyond this is not only curiosity but great rashness.

33. You are not to believe that which you hear in a supernatural way, but only that which you learn through the teaching of Christ and His ministers.

34. The soul that seeks after revelations sins venially at least ; so does the director who encourages or allows that seeking, be the end sought never so good ; there is no necessity at all for this, seeing that we have our natural reason and the evangelical law to guide us in all things.

35. The soul that desires revelations undermines the perfect guidance of the faith, and opens a door for Satan to deceive it by false revelations ; for he knows well how to disguise them so as to make them appear good.

36. The wisdom of the saints consists in knowing

how to direct the will courageously to God, in the perfect fulfilment of His law and His holy counsels.

HOPE

37. That which moves and overcomes God is earnest Hope ; in order to attain to the union of love, the soul must journey in hope of God alone ; for without it nothing will be obtained.

38. A living hope in God makes the soul so courageous and so earnest in the pursuit of the things of everlasting life, that it looks on this world—so indeed it is—as dry, weak, valueless, and dead, in comparison with that it hopes for hereafter.

39. The soul in hope strips itself of all the trappings of this world, setting the heart upon nothing, hoping for nothing in it or of it, clad in the vesture of the hope of everlasting life.

40. Through a living hope in God the heart is so raised up above the world and delivered from all its snares, that not only it cannot come into contact with it, and be attached to it, but it cannot even regard it.

41. In all your trials have recourse at once to God with confidence, and you will be comforted, enlightened, and instructed.

42. The soul that retains the slightest desire for

13

earthly things, is more unseemly and impure in the way of God than if it were labouring under the heaviest and most impure temptations and darkness, provided the rational will did not consent to them ; such a soul may, with greater confidence, draw near to God in obedience to the divine will ; for our Lord hath said : Come unto Me all you who labour and are heavily burdened, and I will refresh you.

43. Have an earnest desire that God may give you all He knows you to be deficient in, for His greater honour and glory.

44. Have a continual trust in God, esteeming in yourself and in your brethren that which He most esteems ; namely, spiritual graces.

45. The more God gives, the more He makes us desire ; until He leaves us empty that He may fill us with good things.

46. So pleased is God with the hope in which the soul is ever looking unto Him with eyes turned away from everything else, that it may be truly said of it that it obtains all that it hopes for.

FEAR OF GOD

47. If you have sweetness and delight, draw near to God in fear and in truth, and you will never be deceived nor entangled in vanity.

48. Do not rejoice in temporal prosperity, because you do not certainly know that it makes eternal life secure.

49. Though a man prosper in all his undertakings, and though every wish of his heart may be gratified, he ought in such a case to fear rather than rejoice ; for this multiplies the occasions of forgetting God, and the risks of offending Him.

50. Do not presume upon vain joy ; knowing how many and how grievous are the sins you have committed, and not knowing whether you are pleasing unto God. But always fear and always hope in Him.

51. How can you venture to live without fear, seeing that you must appear before God to give an account of your lightest words and thoughts ?

52. Remember that the called are many, the chosen few ; and if you are not careful, your final ruin is more certain than your salvation ; especially as the way that leadeth to eternal life is so strait.

53. As in the hour of death you will certainly be sorry that you have not employed all your time in the service of God, why is it that you do not now so employ your time, as you will wish you had done when you are dying.

CHARITY

54. The strength of the soul lies in its faculties, passions, and desires ; if these be directed towards God by the will, and withdrawn from all that is not God, the soul then keeps its strength for Him and loves Him with all its might, as our Lord commands us.

55. Charity is like a fine robe of many colours, which lends grace, beauty, and freshness, not only to the white garment of faith and the green vesture of hope, but also to all the virtues ; for without charity no virtue is pleasing in the sight of God.

56. The worth of love does not consist in high feelings, but in detachment : in patience under all trials for the sake of God Whom we love.

57. God has a greater esteem for the lowest degree of purity of conscience, than for the greatest work you can do for Him.

58. To seek God in Himself is to be without every consolation for His sake ; an inclination to the choice of all that is most unpleasing, whether in the things of God or in the things of the world ; this is to love God.

59. Do not imagine that God is pleased with many good works, so much as with the doing of them with a good will, without self-seeking or human respect.

60. Herein a man may know whether he really loves God : is he satisfied with anything less than God ?

61. As the hair which is frequently dressed is the cleaner, and is the more easily dressed upon all occasions, so is it with the soul which frequently examines its thoughts, words, and works, doing all things for the love of God.

62. As the hair is to be dressed from the top of the head if it is to be thoroughly cleansed, so our good works must have their beginning in the highest love of God, if they are to be thoroughly pure and clean.

63. To restrain the tongue and the thoughts, and to set the affections regularly upon God, quickly sets the soul on fire in a divine way.

64. Study always to please God ; pray that His will may be accomplished in you ; love Him much, for it is His due. (See 311.)

65. All our goodness is a loan : God is the owner ; God worketh, and His work is God.

66. We gain more by the goods of God in one hour, than in our whole life by our own.

67. Our Lord has always manifested the treasures of His wisdom and His Spirit to men ; but now that wickedness manifests itself the more, He manifests them still more.

68. In one sense the purification of a soul from the contradictions of desire is a greater work of God than its creation out of nothing ; that nothing offered no resistance to His Majesty : not so the love of the creature.

69. That which God intends is to make us God by participation, He being God by nature : as the fire changes everything into fire.

70. At the close of life you will be examined as to your love : learn then to love God as He wishes to be loved, and give up all that is your own.

71. The soul that seeks God wholly, must give itself wholly to Him.

72. New and imperfect lovers are like new wine, easily spoiled until the scum of imperfections has been cleared away, and the fervour with the coarse satisfaction of sense has died out.

73. The passions rule over the soul and assail it in proportion to the weakness of the will in God, and to its dependence on creatures ; for then it rejoices so easily in things which do not deserve to be rejoiced in ; hopes for that which is of no profit, and grieves over that in which perhaps it ought to rejoice, and fears where there is nothing to be afraid of.

74. They provoke the divine Majesty to anger exceedingly, who, while seeking for spiritual food, are not

content with God only, but will intermingle therewith carnal and earthly satisfactions.

75. He who loves any other thing together with God makes light of Him, because he puts into the balance with Him that which is at an infinite distance from Him.

76. As a sick man is too weak for work, so the soul that is weak in the love of God is also too weak for the practice of perfect virtue.

77. To seek self in God is to seek for comfort and refreshment from God ; that is contrary to the pure love of God.

78. To regard the gifts of God more than God Himself, is a great evil.

79. Many there are who seek their own pleasure and comfort in God, and gifts and graces from Him ; but they who seek to please Him and to give Him something at their own cost—setting their own pleasure aside— are very few.

80. Few spiritual persons—even among those who think themselves most advanced—attain to a perfect resolution in well-doing, for they never entirely lose themselves on some point or other connected with the world or self, despising appearances and the opinions of men, so as to make their good works perfect and in detachment from all things for the sake of Christ.

81. Self-will and self-satisfaction in the works they do so prevail among men, whether ordinary or more advanced Christians, that scarcely one is to be found who works simply for God without looking for some consolation or comfort or other advantage in his work.

82. Some souls call God their Bridegroom and Beloved ; but He is not really beloved by them, because their heart is not whole with Him.

83. What will it profit you if you give God one thing when He asks something else ? Consider what God wills, and do it, for so will you satisfy your heart better than by doing that to which you are inclined yourself.

84. To find all satisfaction in God you must be satisfied with Him only, for in heaven itself, if you did not bend your will to His will, you would never be satisfied ; so is it here, if your heart is set upon anything else.

85. As aromatic spices exposed to the air gradually lose their fragrance and the strength of their perfume, so the soul, not recollected in the love of God alone, loses the heat and vigour of virtue.

86. He who seeks nothing but God walks not in darkness, however mean and poor he may be in his own estimation.

87. For a man to suffer for God is a sign that he has given himself up to Him, and that he loves Him,

88. He who in the midst of dryness and abandonment is painfully anxious about the service of God, and afraid that He does not serve Him, offers Him a sacrifice that pleaseth Him well.

89. When God is really loved, He hears most readily the cry of the soul that loves Him.

90. The soul defends itself against its fleshly enemy by charity ; for where there is a real love of God neither the love of self nor the love of creatures can enter in.

91. The loving soul is meek, gentle, humble, and patient ; the soul that is hardened in self-love hardens itself still more. If Thou, O good Jesus, in Thy love dost not make the soul gentle, it will persist in its natural hardness.

92. The soul that loves is neither wearied nor wearies.

93. Behold the infinite wisdom and the hidden mysteries ; Oh ! the peace, the love, the silence of the divine bosom ; Oh ! the deep science God is teaching there ; it is that which we call anagogic acts—ejaculatory prayer—Oh ! how they set the heart on fire.

94. The perfect love of God cannot subsist without the knowledge of God and of self.

95. Perfect love naturally seeks nothing, and claims nothing, for itself, but all for the beloved ; if this be so with earthly love, how much more with the love of God ?

96. The old friends of God scarcely ever fail Him, because they are raised above all occasions of failure.

97. True love accepts prosperity and adversity with an even spirit, that of joy and delight.

98. The soul that labours to divest itself of all that is not God for God's sake is immediately enlightened, and transformed, in God, in such a way that the soul seems to be God Himself, and to possess the things of God.

99. Satan fears a soul united with God, as he fears God Himself.

100. The soul, in the union of love, resists even the first impulses.

101. Purity of heart is nothing less than the love and grace of God. Hence our Lord says : Blessed are the pure in heart ; that is, those who love ; for blessedness is given to nothing less than love.

102. He who truly loves God is not ashamed before men of what he does for God ; neither does he hide his good works out of shame, though the whole world may condemn them.

103. He who truly loves God thinks it a great gain to lose all he has, and his own life, for God.

104. If the soul had but one glimpse of the beauty of God, not only would it desire to die that it might see Him for ever, but it would joyfully undergo a thou-

sand most bitter deaths to see Him again, if only for a moment.

105. He who acts out of the pure love of God, not only does not perform his actions to be seen of men, but does not do them even that God may know of them. Such an one, if he thought it possible that his good works might escape the eye of God, would still perform them with the same joy, and in the same pureness of love.

106. It is a great matter to be much exercised in love : in order that the soul, made perfect and consummated therein, may not be long detained, either in this life or the next, from the vision of God.

107. A pure and perfect work, wrought for God in a pure heart, makes a perfect kingdom for its Lord.

108. To the pure in heart high things and low are profitable, and minister to their greater purity ; while to the impure, by reason of their impurity, both the one and the other are occasions of greater evil.

109. The pure in heart find in all things the knowledge of God, sweet, chaste, pure, spiritual, joyous and loving.

PEACE

110. By keeping guard over the senses, which are the gates of the soul, we keep also and increase its tranquillity and purity.

111. Man would never lose peace if he forgot and cast aside his thoughts and notions, and withdrew from the sight, hearing, and conversation of men so far as he well may.

112. If we forget all created things, there is then nothing to disturb our peace ; nothing to excite the desires that disturb it ; for, as the proverb says, What the eye hath not seen, the heart doth not desire.

113. The restless and perturbed soul, the passions and desires of which are not wholly mortified, is, as such, incapacited for spiritual good, for that enters only into the soul which is under control and ordered in peace.

114. Be assured of this : God reigns only in the peaceful and unselfish soul.

115. Be tranquil ; put away superfluous thoughts, and make light of whatever may happen ; so shall your service be pleasing unto God, and you shall rejoice in Him.

116. Keep your heart in peace ; let nothing in this world disturb it : all things have an end.

117. Be not made sad by the adverse events of this life, for you know not the good they bring with them, ordained in the judgments of God, for the everlasting joy of the elect.

118. In all circumstances, however hard they may be, we should rejoice, rather than be cast down, that we

may not lose the greatest good, the peace and tranquillity of our soul.

119. If the whole world and all that is in it were thrown into confusion, disquietude on that account would be vanity, because that disquietude would do more harm than good.

120. To endure all things with an equable and peaceful mind, not only brings with it many blessings to the soul, but also enables us, in the midst of our difficulties, to have a clear judgment about them, and to minister the fitting remedy for them.

121. It is not the will of God that the soul should be troubled by anything, or that it should be afflicted ; for if men are afflicted because of the adversities of this world, that is the effect of their being weak in virtue ; for the soul of the perfect rejoices in that which gives pain to the soul of the imperfect.

122. The heavens are stedfast, not subject to generation ; and souls which are of a heavenly nature are stedfast, not subject to the generation of desires, nor of anything of that kind : they are in some measure like unto God, Who never changes.

LOVE OF OUR NEIGHBOUR

123. Wisdom enters by love, silence, and mortification. It is great wisdom to know when to be silent,

when to suffer, and never to regard the sayings, doings, or lives of others.

124. See that you do not intermeddle in the affairs of other people, nor discuss them in your own thoughts; for perhaps you will not be able to fulfil your own task.

125. Suspect no evil of your brother, for that takes away purity of heart.

126. Never listen to accounts of the frailties of others; and if anyone should complain to you of another, humbly ask him not to speak about him at all.

127. Do not shrink from trouble: though it may seem to you more than you can bear. Let all men find you compassionate.

128. No one merits love except for the virtue that he has; and when love is so ordered, it is according to God, and in great freedom.

129. When the love and affection we give to the creature is purely spiritual and founded on God, the love of God grows with it; and the more we remember the earthly love, the more we also remember God and desire Him: the one grows apace with the other.

130. When the love of the creature springs from sensual vice, or from a purely natural inclination, in proportion to its growth is the diminution of the love of God and forgetfulness of Him; and from the recollection of the creature, remorse of conscience comes.

131. That which is born of the flesh is flesh, and that which is born of the spirit is spirit, saith our Saviour in His Gospel. So the love which grows out of sensuality ends in sensuality ; that which is of the spirit ends in the spirit of God, and makes it grow. This is the difference between these two loves, that men may distinguish between them.

DISORDERLY APPETITES

132. He who loves any creature out of the order of charity, becomes vile as that creature itself, and in one sense even viler ; for love not only levels but subjects also the lover to the object of his love.

133. The passions and desires, when under control and restrained, are sources of all virtue, and also, when they have broken loose, of all the vices and imperfections of the soul.

134. Every desire hurts the soul in five ways, beside robbing it of the Spirit of God : 1. It fatigues it. 2. Torments it. 3. Blinds it. 4. Defiles it. 5. Weakens it.

135. All created things are crumbs which fall from the table of God ; and for that reason, they who go about feeding on the creature are rightly called dogs ;

they are, therefore, always hungry like dogs, and justly so, because crumbs excite, rather than appease, hunger.

136. The desires are like restless and dissatisfied children begging of their mother, now one thing, now another, never contented ; like one ill of a burning fever, never at rest, and whose thirst increases while the fever continues.

137. As a man dragging a cart up hill, so is that soul on its way to God, which does not throw aside the cares of this life, and does not deny itself.

138. As he is tormented who falls into the hands of his enemies, so is the soul afflicted and tormented which is carried away by its desires.

139. As a man is tormented and afflicted who lies down naked amid thorns and briars, so is the soul tormented and afflicted which lies down in the midst of its desires : they pierce, torture, and tear it painfully.

140. As vapours darken the air and hide the light of the sun, so the soul, captive to its desires, is, as to the understanding, in darkness, so that neither the sun of natural reason nor that of the supernatural wisdom of God can reach it or enlighten it.

141. He who feeds his desires is like a moth, or a fish dazzled by the light which the fishermen throw over the water, that it may not see the ruin which the fishermen have prepared for it.

142. Who can tell how impossible it is for the soul, subject to desires, to judge of the things of God ? for while the film of desire is over the eye of its judgment, it sees nothing but that film, now of one colour, now of another ; and so it comes to regard the things of God as not the things of God, and those which are not the things of God as the things of God.

143. A bird that has perched upon a twig covered with birdlime labours in a twofold way, in setting itself free, and in cleaning itself ; so a soul, that has given way to desires ; it has to set itself free in the first place, and then to clean itself of that which has clung to it.

144. As soot defiles the most beautiful and perfect face, so the unruly desires of the soul defile and pollute that soul which entertains them, and yet that soul in itself is the most beautiful and perfect image of God.

145. He that toucheth pitch, saith the Holy Ghost, shall be defiled with it.* A soul touches pitch when it satisfies the desires of the will in any created thing.

146. If my object were to describe the foul and corrupt condition to which the desires reduce the soul, I should not be able to find anything so full of cobwebs and worms, not even corruption itself wherewith to compare it.

* Ecclus. xiii. 1.

14

147. The desires are like the suckers which grow on a tree, they sap its strength and destroy its fertility.

148. There are corrupt humours which so weaken a man's gait, and make him loathe his food, as the desire of the creature weakens the soul, indisposing it for the practice of virtue.

149. Many souls have no inclination for virtue, because their desires are not pure, and not for God.

150. As the young vipers, growing in the womb, feed on their mother and kill her, preserving their own lives at the cost of hers, so the unmortified desires prey on the soul and kill in it the life of God ; they at last are the only things that live in it, because the soul has not killed them first.

151. As it is necessary to till the earth that it may bring forth fruit—for otherwise it will produce nothing but weeds,—so also is it necessary to mortify our desires, that the soul may be clean.

152. As wood is never transformed into fire if but one degree of heat necessary for that end be wanting, so the soul that has one imperfection can never be perfectly transformed in God.

153. Whether it be a strong wire rope, or a slender and delicate thread, that holds the bird, it matters not if it really detains it, for, until the cord be broken, the bird cannot fly ; so the soul, held in the bonds of human

affections, however slight they may be, cannot, while they last, make its way to God.

154. The desires and attachments of the soul have the property attributed to the remora, which, though it be but a very little fish, yet it arrests the progress of the ship to which it clings.

155. O that spiritual men knew how they are losing the blessings and fulness of the Spirit, merely because they will not raise up their desires above trifles ! and how they might have the sweetness of all things in the pure food of the Spirit—of which the manna was a figure—if they would only abstain from tasting other food.

156. The children of Israel did not find in the manna all the sweetness and strength they might have found in it ; not because the manna did not contain them, but because they longed for other meat.

157. Of one spark cometh a great fire, and one imperfection is enough to beget others. We shall never see a soul negligent in resisting but one single desire, which has not many other desires, springing out of that weakness and imperfection from which the first proceeds.

158. Voluntary and perfectly deliberate desires, however slight they may be, if only habitual, are those which chiefly hinder our progress to perfection.

159. Any imperfection to which the soul is attached

and accustomed, is a greater injury to virtue than a daily fall into many other and even greater imperfections, provided they do not result from the habitual indulgence of an evil inclination.

160. God is justly angry with certain souls whom He, by His mighty arm, has delivered from the world, and from the occasions of grievous sins, but who are weak and negligent in mortifying certain imperfections ; for this He permits them to fall through their desires from bad to worse.

PRUDENCE

161. Give heed to reason, that you may perform that which it dictates to you in the way of God : and it will serve you more than all good works heedlessly done, and all the spiritual sweetness you aim at.

162. Blessed is he who, setting his own tastes and inclinations aside, looks at things according to reason and justice, in order to accomplish them.

163. He who acts according to reason is as one who eats strong and substantial food ; but he who in his works seeks the satisfaction of his own will, is as one who eats poor and unripe fruit.

164. No creature may transgress the limits which God has set for it in the order of its nature : and as He

has appointed for man's governance certain natural and rational laws, the transgression thereof, by seeking knowledge in a supernatural way, is neither holy nor becoming : moreover, God is displeased ; and if at any time He vouchsafes an answer, it is out of condescension to the soul's weakness.

165. Man knows not how to order his joy and grief reasonably and prudently, because he knows not the distance between good and evil.

166. We know not how to distinguish between our right hand and our left : for at every step we take evil for good and good for evil, and if this be as it were natural to us, what must it be if desire be added to our natural blindness.

167. The desire, as desire, is blind, because in itself it regards not reason, which is that which ever guides and directs the soul aright in its operations : so the soul, whenever it is guided by its desires, is blind.

THE ANGELS

168. The angels are our shepherds, because they carry not only our message to God, but also those of God to our souls, feeding them with sweet inspirations and divine communications : as good shepherds they protect

us, and defend us from the wolves, which are the evil spirits.

169. Through the secret inspirations which the angels convey to the soul, they effect a deeper knowledge of God, and make it love Him the more, till they leave it wounded with love.

170. The divine wisdom which in heaven illumines the angels, and cleanses them of their ignorances, is the same which illumines men upon earth, and cleanses them of their errors and imperfections; it flows from God through the first orders of the hierarchies down to the lowest, and thence to men.

171. The light of God, which illumines an angel, enlightening and setting him on fire with love, as pure spirit disposed for that inflowing, illumines man ordinarily in darkness, pain, and distress, because of his impurity and weakness: so is the sun to a weak eye the light it gives is painful.

172. When man has become spiritualised and refined in the fire of divine love which purifies him, he is then within the union and inflowing of the loving illumination with the sweetness with which an angel receives them. There are souls who in this life receive a more perfect illumination than the angels.

173. When God gives great graces to a soul through the hands of an angel, He ordinarily allows the devil

to know it, that he may assail that soul with all his might, according to the measure of justice, in order that the victory may be the more prized, and the soul, faithful in temptation, may be the more abundantly rewarded.

174. Remember that your guardian angel does not always move the will to act, though he always enlightens the reason ; therefore do not promise yourself sensible sweetness always in your works, because reason and understanding are sufficient.

175. When the desires of man are occupied with anything that is not God, they embarrass the soul and shut the door against the light by which the angel moves it to virtue.

176. Consider what utter vanity it is to rejoice in anything but in the service of God, how dangerous and how fatal ; how ruinous it proved to the angels who rejoiced and had complacency in their own beauty and their natural endowments ; for this they fell deformed into the abyss.

A SPIRITUAL DIRECTOR

177. A soul without a director is like a kindled coal, which, left by itself, cools instead of burning.

178. He who insists on being left to himself, without a director to guide him, is like an unowned tree by the wayside ; however fruitful it may be, the travellers pick its fruit, and none of it ripens.

179. The tree that is cultivated and kept carefully by its owner produces fruit in due season, and the owner is not disappointed.

180. He who falls alone remains alone in his fall ; he makes little account of his soul, because he trusts in himself alone.

181. He who is carrying a burden when he falls, rises with difficulty under his burden.

182. He who falls, being blind, cannot rise, being blind and alone ; and if he should rise by himself, he will walk in a direction that is not good for him.

183. If you are not afraid to fall by yourself, how can you venture to raise yourself alone ? Remember that two are better than one.

184. Our Lord did not say in His gospel, where one is by himself there am I, but where there are at the least two : this is to show that no one should believe of himself, or confirm himself in, the things which he thinks are those of God, without the counsel and direction of the Church and her ministers.

185. Woe to him that is alone, saith the Holy Ghost ; and therefore the soul has need of a director, for both

will resist the devil more easily, being both together to learn and practise the truth.

186. It is the will of God that the government of one man should be in the hands of another, and that we should not give perfect credit to those matters which He communicates supernaturally Himself, until they shall have passed through the human channel of another man's mouth.

187. When God makes a particular revelation to a soul, he also inclines that soul to make it known to the minister of His Church, who stands in His place.

188. It is not every one who is fitted for the direction of souls ; it being a matter of the last importance to give right or wrong advice in so serious a matter as that.

189. Let the soul that would advance, and not go back, take care into whose hands it commits itself ; for, as the master, so the scholar, and as the father, so the child.

190. The inclinations and tastes of the director are easily impressed upon the penitent.

191. The chief solicitude of spiritual directors should be to mortify every desire of their penitents : to make them deny themselves in all they desire, so as to deliver them from so great misery.

192. However high the doctrine, adorned the elo-

quence, sublime the style, the fruits of the sermon will be, in general, no better than the spirit of the preacher.

193. A good style and action, high doctrines and correct expression, have a greater effect when accompanied by true spirituality ; but without that the will is scarcely or but little inflamed, though the senses may be charmed and the understanding delighted.

194. God is angry with those who teach His law and keep it not ; and who preach spirituality to others without being spiritual themselves.

195. For the highest parts, and even for the ordinary parts, of the way of perfection, you will scarcely find one capable guide throughout, such as men have need of : such an one must be wise, discreet, and experienced.

196. For though the foundations of direction be knowledge and discretion, yet if directors be without experience, they will never be able to guide the soul in the way in which God is leading it ; they will make it go backwards, ordering it after low methods which they pick up in books.

197. He who shall presumptuously err in the direction of souls, being under obligation to give good counsel —as every one is in the office he undertakes—shall not escape punishment according to the evil he has done ; for the work of God—and such is the direction of souls —demands great caution and counsel.

198. Who can be like St. Paul, who was all things to all, that he might save all? knowing all the ways by which God leads souls, which are so different one from another, that you can scarcely find one which in half its ways agrees with the ways of another.

RELIGION, PRAYER

199. The greatest honour we can render unto God, is to serve Him in evangelical perfection : and whatever is beside this is of no value or advantage to man.

200. One thought of man is of more value than the whole world ; God alone is, for that reason, the worthy object of it, and to Him alone is it due ; every thought of man, therefore, which is not given to God, is a robbery.

201. In all nature there are correspondences ; insensible things correspond with those that are insensible ; sense with things sensible ; and man's thoughts with the Spirit of God.

NECESSITY OF PRAYER

202. Never let your heart waste its affections, not even for a moment.

203. The soul cannot overcome the devil without

prayer, nor penetrate his devices without humility and mortification : for the weapons of God are prayer and the Cross of Christ.

204. In all our necessities, trials, and afflictions, there is no better nor safer remedy than prayer, and hope that God will provide for us in His own way.

FRUITS OF PRAYER

205. Let God be the Bridegroom and the beloved of your soul ; remain always in His presence, and so you shall avoid sin, learn to love Him, and all things will prosper with you.

206. Enter into your innermost heart, and labour in the presence of God, the Bridegroom of the soul, Who is ever present doing you good.

207. Strive to be continually in the presence of God, and to preserve the purity which He teaches.

208. By prayer aridity is expelled, devotion increased, and the interior practice of virtue is established in the soul.

209. By shutting the eyes to the defects of others, keeping silence, and conversing continually with God, great imperfections are rooted out of your soul, which thereby becomes possessed of great virtues.

210. When prayer is made in the pure and simple

understanding of God, it seems to the soul to have lasted but a moment, though in fact it occupied much time ; this is that prayer of a moment, of which it is said that it pierces the clouds.

THE PROPERTIES OF PRAYER

211. The powers and senses of the soul should not be employed altogether upon anything unless it be a matter which cannot be neglected ; for the rest, they should be unoccupied for God.

212. Wait lovingly upon God, without any desire to feel or understand anything in particular of Him.

213. Strive to attain to that state in which nothing is of importance to you, and you of importance to none, so that being utterly forgotten you may be with God in secret.

214. He who will not allow his desires to carry him away will wing his flight like a bird whose wings are strong.

215. Do not nourish your soul upon anything else but on God : repel the remembrance of things, let peace and recollection fill your heart.

216. If you would attain to holy recollection, it must be by rejecting, and not by admitting.

217. Seek by reading and you will find by meditat-

ing ; cry in prayer and the door will be opened in contemplation.

218. True devotion and spirituality consist in perseverance in prayer, with patience and humility, distrust-
ing yourself that you may please God only.

219. They call upon God in truth who pray for that
which is most true : namely, that which belongs to their
eternal salvation.

220. There is no better way to obtain the desires of
our heart than to pray with all our might for that which
is most pleasing unto God ; for then He will grant us not
only our salvation, which we pray for, but also that
which He sees expedient for us, though we may never
ask for it, and though it may have never entered into
our hearts to do so.

221. Let every soul understand that, although God
may not succour it in its necessities when it cries, He
will not however fail it when the time comes ; provided
it does not lose heart and cease from prayer.

MOTIVES FOR PRAYER

222. When the will, the moment it feels any joy in
sensible things, rises upwards in that joy to God, and
when sensible things move it to pray, it should not reject

them, it may and should make use of them for so holy
an exercise ; because sensible things, under these conditions, subserve the end for which God created them :
namely, to be occasions of making Him better known
and loved.

223. He whose senses are subject to the Spirit,
purged from all sensible objects, even in his first movements, elicits delight in the sweet knowledge and contemplation of God.

224. As it is a truth of sound philosophy that the
life of every creature is in harmony with its constitution,
so is it clear beyond all contradiction, that he whose life
is spiritual—the animal life being mortified—must be
wholly tending towards God.

225. The will of a devout person rests chiefly on the
invisible ; he requires but few images for his use, and
these are such as are more conformable to divine, than
to human, taste, ordering himself herein after the ways
of the other world, and not of this.

226. The chief thing to be regarded in images is
devotion and faith ; if these be absent, the image will not
be sufficient. What a perfect living image our Lord
was upon earth, and yet those who had no faith, though
they were about Him, and saw His wonderful works,
were none the better.

PLACE FOR PRAYER

227. Keep yourself apart for one thing only, that which brings everything with it ; solitude, accompanied by prayer and spiritual reading : and there abide, forgetting all things, if there be no obligation upon you to remember them. You will please God more by keeping watch over, and perfecting, yourself, than if you gained everything : for what doth it profit a man if he gain the whole world, if he loses his own soul ?

228. Pure spirituality gives no heed to matters which do not concern it, or to human respect ; but alone and apart from all created forms, communicates interiorly in sweet tranquillity with God ; for the knowledge of Him lies in a divine silence.

229. For the purposes of prayer that place is to be chosen in which sense and spirit may be least hindered from rising upwards unto God.

230. The place of prayer must not be pleasant and delectable to the senses—some people seek such a place —lest the issue should be recreation of sense, and not recollection of spirit.

231. He who goes on a pilgrimage will do well to do so when others do not, though it be at an unusual season. When pilgrims are many, I would advise stay-

ing at home, for in general men return more dissipated than they were before they went. They who become pilgrims for recreation, rather than devotion, are many in number.

HINDRANCES TO PRAYER

232. He who interrupts the course of his spiritual exercises and prayer, is like a man who allows a bird to escape from his hand ; he can hardly catch it again.

233. God being, as He is, inaccessible, do not rest on the consideration of objects perceptible by sense, and comprehended by the understanding. This is to be satisfied with what is less than God ; so doing you will destroy that energy of the soul which is necessary for walking with Him.

234. Never admit into your soul that which is not substantially spiritual ; for if you do so you will lose the sweetness of devotion and recollection.

235. He who relies much on sense will never be very spiritual ; they deceive themselves who think they can, in the sheer strength of our grovelling senses, attain to the power of the spirit.

236. The imperfect destroy true devotion, because they seek sensible sweetness in prayer.

15

237. The fly that touches the honey cannot fly ; so the soul that clings to spiritual sweetness ruins its freedom and hinders contemplation.

238. He who will not dispose himself to pray in every place, but only there where his own taste is gratified, will frequently fail in his prayer ; because, as they say, he can pray only in his own parish.

239. He who is not conscious of liberty of spirit amid the things of sense and sweetness, which should serve as motives to prayer, and whose will rests and feeds upon them, ought to abstain from the use of them, for to him they are a hindrance on the road to God.

240. It is very foolish, when spiritual sweetness and delight fail, to imagine that God has failed us also ; and to imagine, that because we have such sweetness, that we have God also.

241. Very often many spiritual persons employ their senses upon sensible things, under the pretext of giving themselves to prayer, and raising their hearts to God ; now this that they do should be called recreation rather than prayer ; pleasing themselves rather than God.

242. Meditation tends to contemplation, as means to an end. So when the end is attained, the means are laid aside ; men rest at the end of their journey ; thus, when the state of contemplation has been attained, meditation must cease.

243. As it is necessary, at the proper time, to give up the work of reflection and meditation in order to draw near unto God, lest it should prove an impediment, so also is it necessary not to give it up before the time lest we should go back.

244. There are three signs of contemplation and interior recollection of the soul : 1. When the soul takes no pleasure in transitory things. 2. When it seeks solitude and silence, striving after that which is the more perfect. 3. When meditation, which was once a help, proves a hindrance. These three signs must be found together.

245. In the beginning of the state of contemplation the loving knowledge of God is, as it were, imperceptible : in the first place, because it is most subtile and delicate, and, as it were, imperceptible ; in the second place, because the soul has been accustomed to the practice of meditation, which is more cognisable by the senses.

246. The more the soul is disposed for tranquillity, the more will the loving knowledge of contemplation grow ; the soul will feel it and relish it more than all other things whatever ; because it brings with it peace and rest, sweetness and delight, without trouble.

247. They who have entered the state of contemplation, must not for that reason suppose that they are never to make a meditation any more ; for in the be-

ginning the habit of it is not so established that they can have it whenever they will; neither are they so far removed from meditation as to be unable to meditate as they were accustomed to do.

248. Except in the act of contemplation, in all exercises and good works, the soul must make use of memory and good meditations in such a way as to increase devotion and profit, particularly dwelling on the life, passion, and death of our Lord Jesus Christ, in order that its works, exercises, and life may be conformed to His.

249. The conditions of the ' solitary sparrow ' are five : 1. It ascends as high as it can. 2. It admits none to be its companion, even of its own kind. 3. It faces the wind. 4. It has no definite colour. 5. It sings sweetly. The contemplative soul should be like it ; it must rise high above transitory things, making no more account of them than if they never existed ; it must be so enamoured of solitude and silence as to suffer no creature to be in its company ; it must face the wind of the Holy Ghost, corresponding to His inspirations, that so doing, it may become more worthy of His company ; it must have no definite colour, bent upon nothing but on doing the will of God ; it must sing sweetly in the contemplation and love of God.

250. Though occasionally, in the height of contem-

plation and simple view of the divinity, the soul may not remember the most sacred humanity of Christ, because God elevates the spirit to knowledge, the most supernatural, yet studiously to forget it is in nowise seemly, seeing that by the contemplation thereof, and loving meditation thereon, the soul will ascend to the highest state of union ; for Christ our Lord is the truth, the gate, the way, and the guide to all good.

OBEDIENCE

251. The way of life demands little trouble and care, it demands denial of the will rather than much knowledge ; he who inclines to pleasure and sweetness will be the less able to travel on it.

252. He who does not walk in the way of his own pleasure, nor in that of the pleasures which come from God, nor in that of those which come from creatures, and never does his own will, he shall never stumble.

253. Though you may undertake great things, yet, if you will not learn to deny your own will and to be obedient, casting away all anxiety about yourself and your own affairs, you will make no progress in the way of perfection.

254. Let others teach you, let others order you, let others rule over you, and you will become perfect.

255. God is more pleased with that soul which, in spiritual aridity and trouble, is subject and obedient, than with that which, without obedience, performs all its duties in great spiritual sweetness.

256. God would rather have from you the lowest degree of obedience and subjection, than all those services you attempt to render Him.

257. Subjection and obedience is the penance of reason and discretion ; and therefore a more pleasing and acceptable sacrifice in the eyes of God than all other bodily penances.

258. Bodily penance, without obedience, is a most imperfect thing ; beginners practise it out of a desire for it, and for the pleasure they find in it, and therefore, because they herein do their own will, grow in vice, rather than in virtue.

259. Inasmuch as a double bitterness results from fulfilling one's own will ; do not fulfil it, although it may be bitterness to remain quiet.

260. The devil prevails with ease over those who are alone, and who in the things of God order themselves according to their own will.

FORTITUDE, PATIENCE

261. It is better when burdened to be with the strong, than unburdened with the weak. When you are

loaded with afflictions you are with God, Who is your strength, and He is with the afflicted. When you are unburdened you are by yourself, who are weakness itself, for the virtue and fortitude of the soul grow and are made strong in tribulations.

262. Your flesh is weak, and no worldly thing can strengthen or comfort your spirit ; that which is born of the world is worldly, and that which is born of flesh is flesh : a good spirit is born only of the Spirit of God, and is communicated neither through the world nor the flesh.

263. The most delicate flower is the first to wither, and to lose its fragrance : therefore take care you do not walk in the way of spiritual sweetness, for you will never be firm. Choose rather a strong spirit, attached to nothing, and you will find sweetness and abundance of peace. Savoury, sweet, and lasting fruit is gathered only in a dry and cold soil.

264. Though the road be plain and pleasant for men of good will, he who travels on it will travel little, and that with difficulty, if not possessed of courage, strength, and resolution.

265. Feed not in forbidden pastures, which are those of this life : the blessed are they who hunger and thirst after justice, for they shall be filled.

266. Verily he has overcome all things in whom

pleasure in them excites no joy, and the bitterness of them no sadness.

267. By fortitude the soul labours, practises virtue, and overcomes vice.

268. Let your heart be strong against everything that may draw you to that which is not God, and be at home in the sufferings of Christ.

269. Rejoice in God always, for He is your salvation, and consider how blessed it is to suffer whatever may come from Him who is the true good.

270. If you incline to aridities and suffering for the love of God, He will esteem that in you of more value than all the spiritual visions, meditations, and consolations you may ever have.

271. Never, for good or for evil, suffer your heart to be otherwise than calm in the affections of love ; that you may endure whatever may befall you.

272. We are not to measure our trials by ourselves, but ourselves by our trials.

273. If souls knew how much suffering and mortification help to the attainment of great blessings, they would never seek for consolation anywhere.

274. If a soul has more patience under suffering, a greater endurance in the absence of sweetness, that is a sign of greater progress in virtue.

275. The way of suffering is more secure and also

more profitable than that of joy and action. In suffering, the strength of God is given to the soul, while in
joy and action it has to do with its own weakness and
imperfections : in suffering also virtues are acquired
and practised ; the soul is purified, and is rendered more
prudent and cautious.

276. The soul that is not tried and proved in temptations and afflictions can never attain unto wisdom, as
it is written in the book Ecclesiasticus : ' What doth
he know that hath not been tried ? ' *

277. The most perfect suffering brings with it the
most perfect understanding.

MODESTY

278. The soul, by refraining from joy in the objects
of sense, recovers itself from the distractions into which
it has fallen through the excessive indulgence of the
senses, and recollects itself in God : spirituality and the
virtues it has acquired are also preserved and increased.

279. As the man who seeks pleasure in the things of
sense, and rejoices in them, ought not, and deserves not,
to be called by any other name than sensual, animal,
and earthly, so he whose joy is beyond and above these

* Ecclus. xxxiv. 9.

things, merits the name of spiritual, heavenly, and divine.

280. If you will deny yourself one joy in the things of sense, our Lord will repay you a hundredfold in this life, spiritually and temporally; and for one joy indulged in the things of sense, you shall have a hundred sorrows and afflictions.

281. All the functions and powers of his senses, who no longer lives after the flesh, are directed to divine contemplation.

282. Though the goods of sense may deserve to be somewhat rejoiced in when they help a man to raise his thoughts to God, yet this is so uncertain that in general they do a man more harm than good.

283. Until a man shall have so habituated his senses to the purgation from sensible joy, that all things raise him up to God, he must refrain from all joy in them, in order that he may wean his soul from the life of sense.

SILENCE

284. The Father uttered one Word; that Word is His Son: and He utters Him for ever in everlasting silence, and in silence the soul has to hear It.

285. That which we most require for our spiritual

growth is the silence of the desire and of the tongue before God, Who is so high : the language He most listens to is that of silent love.

286. Speak little : and do not meddle in matters when you are not desired to do so.

287. Never listen to accounts of the frailties of others ; and if any one should complain to you of another, humbly ask him not to speak about him at all.

288. Complain of no one : ask for nothing, but if it should be necessary to ask, do so in few words.

289. Abstain from contradiction : on no account let your words be other than pure.

290. Let your words be offensive to none ; and about matters that will cause you no trouble if everybody knew of them.

291. Preserve your spirit in peace, lovingly attentive to God : and when you must speak, do so calmly and peaceably.

292. Be silent about what God may say to you, remembering the words of Scripture : ' My secret to me.' *

293. Never forget that of every word uttered without the direction of obedience, God will require a strict account.

294. Intercourse with people beyond what is strictly

* Is. xxiv. 16.

necessary, and required by reason, has never been good for any man, however holy he may have been.

295. It is impossible to make progress otherwise than by doing and suffering everything in silence.

296. For growth in virtue, the important thing is to be silent, and to work : conversation distracts, silence and work bring recollection.

297. The moment a person understands what is told him for his good, there is no necessity. for him to ask for further direction, nor to speak about it, but to act upon it sincerely in silence, carefully, in humility, charity, and contempt of self.

298. I have understood that the soul which is ready for talking and the commerce of the world is but little attentive to God: for if it were otherwise, it would withdraw itself at once into silence within, and avoid all conversation whatever.

299. It is the will of God that the soul should delight in Him, rather than in any created thing, however useful or necessary it may be to it.

HUMILITY

300. The first thing the soul must have in order to attain to the knowledge of God is the knowledge of itself.

301. God is more pleased with certain actions, however few they may be, done in silence and in secret, and without any desire that men might see them, than with a thousand grand actions undertaken with the intention of their being seen by men.

302. The secrecy of conscience is broken when a man reveals to others the good estate it is in, receiving for his reward the praise of men.

303. The Wise Spirit of God Who dwells in humble souls inclines them to keep His treasures in secret, and to cast out what is amiss.

304. Perfection consists not in those virtues which every one recognises in himself, but in those which God approves of. And as His approval is hidden from the eyes of men, no one has any reason to presume, and every one many, to make him afraid.

305. God, when He loves a soul, regards not its greatness, but rather the greatness of its contempt of self and its humility.

306. What you most seek, and most anxiously desire, you will never find if you seek it for yourself, not even in the most profound contemplation ; but only in deep humility and submission of heart.

307. If you will glory in yourself, cast away everything not your own : what remains will be nothing, and thing you should glory in.

308. Do not despise others because, as it seems to you, they do not possess the virtues you thought they had : they may be pleasing to God for other reasons which you cannot discover.

309. Never excuse yourself : listen calmly to the reprimand and consider it to come from God.

310. Look upon it as a special mercy of God, that people ever speak kindly to you : you do not deserve it.

311. Make neither much nor little of him who may be against you, and strive always to please God. Pray that His will may be done, and love Him much, for it is His due.

312. Love to be unknown to yourself and others : never regard the good nor the evil of others.

313. Never forget the life to come. Consider how many in heaven are great, and in great glory, who in their own eyes were of no account, humble and poor.

314. In order to mortify truly the desire of honour from which so many other desires proceed, you will do those things which will bring you into contempt, and you will wish others to despise you : you will speak disparagingly of yourself and you will contrive that others do so : you will think humbly and contemptuously of yourself, and you will wish others to do so also.

315. Humility and submission to your spiritual director, disclosing to him all that passes in your inter-

course with God, will bring light, rest, contentment, and security.

316. Virtue consists not in what you have learned, and feel about God, however great that may be, nor in any personal experiences of this kind, but, on the contrary, in that which is not matter of feeling at all, in great humility, contempt of self, and of all that belongs to you profoundly rooted in the soul.

317. All visions, revelations, and impressions of heaven, however much the spiritual man may esteem them, are not equal in worth to the least act of humility : for this brings forth the fruits of charity, which never esteems nor thinks well of self, but only of others.

318. The communications which come really from God have this property, that they humble and exalt the soul at the same time, for in the way of the Spirit to descend is to ascend, and to ascend is to descend.

319. When God communicates His gifts and graces to the soul, He excites in it a repugnance to accept honours and distinctions ; but in the way of humility and self-abasement, He gives it ease and readiness.

320. God hates to see men ready to accept dignities, even when it is His will that they should accept them ; but it is not His will that they should do so eagerly and promptly.

321. When the devil speaks, he makes men ready

and eager to accept dignities, but he makes them reject humiliations and self-abasement.

VANITY

322. He who loves superiorities and dignities, or the indulgence of his desires, stands before God, not as a son who is free, but as one of mean condition, and slave of his passions.

323. The soul that is not humble, the devil most easily deludes, and makes it believe a thousand lies.

324. There are many Christians in our day who have certain virtues, and who do great things, but all of no use to them in the matter of everlasting life, because in them they do not seek that honour and glory which belongs to God alone, but rather the empty satisfaction of their own will.

325. Empty joy in our good works is always attended by a great esteem of them ; out of this comes boasting, and other faults such as we see in the Pharisee in the gospel.

326. Such is the misery of the children of men, that, so far as I can see, the greater part of their good works done in public are either sinful or worthless ; or imperfect and defective in the sight of God, because men

will not detach themselves from self-interest and from human respect.

327. O souls created for, and called unto, a dignity so great ! what are you doing, what is it that detains you ? O miserable blindness of the children of Adam, who in a light so great are blind, and to such an invitation deaf ! While they seek after greatness and honour they are themselves miserable and base, and of such blessings unworthy.

VOLUNTARY POVERTY

328. If rejoicing in riches can be made in any way endurable, it is when men spend and use them in the service of God ; there is no other way of making them profitable : the same principle applies to all other temporal goods, titles, rank and office.

329. The spiritual man must be very careful of the beginnings of joy in temporal things, lest from little it should become great, increasing step by step ; out of slight beginnings great evils result. One spark is enough to set a mountain on fire.

330. However small an attachment may be, be not too confident that you can cut it off at any time ; cut it off at once : for if you have not the courage to destroy

16

it when it is but beginning, how can you presume upon success when it has taken root and grown ?

331. He who turns aside from what is little, will not stumble over what is large. Little matters cause great evils, because the fences and walls of the heart are broken down when they enter in ; for the proverb says : he who has begun his work has accomplished the half of it.

332. Joy darkens the judgment as a cloud, for there can be no rejoicing in created things without the attachment of the will. The negation and purgation of this joy leave the judgment clear as the sky when the mist has been scattered.

333. He who is detached is not molested when he prays, nor at any other time, and so without wasting his time he gains with ease great spiritual treasures.

AVARICE

334. Although temporal goods are not, in themselves, necessarily, occasions of sin, yet ordinarily, by reason of our frailty, the heart of man sets its affections upon them, and falls away from God, which is sin : for this reason the Wise Man saith : the rich shall not be free from sin.*

335. The things of this world neither occupy nor

* Ecclus. xi. 10.

injure the soul ; it is not they that enter into it, but rather the will, and the desire of them, which dwell within it.

336. Our Lord Jesus Christ, in the gospel, calls riches thorns, giving us to understand that he who sets his will upon them shall be wounded by sin.

337. It is vanity to desire to have children, as some do, who weary the world with their fretting for them : they know not if their children will be good, and servants of God : neither do they know whether the pleasure they expect from them may not be turned into disquietude, pain, and trouble.

338. The covetous man runs to and fro within the limits of the chain by which his heart is bound, and with all his efforts can scarcely set himself free, even for a moment, from the bondage of his thoughts on which his heart is set.

POVERTY OF SPIRIT

339. Consider how very necessary it is for you to set your face against yourself, and walk in the way of penance if you would attain to perfection.

340. If any one tempts you with lax opinions, and should even confirm them by miracles, trust him not ; but rely rather upon penance and perfect detachment from creatures.

341. God in His law commanded the altar of sacrifice should be empty within. This is to teach us that He would have the soul emptied of all things, that it may be an altar worthy of His Majesty.

342. One desire only does God allow, and suffer in His presence within the soul—the desire of keeping the law perfectly, and carrying the cross of Christ. It is not said, in the sacred writings, that God commanded anything to be laid up in the ark with the manna except the book of the law and the rod of Moses, a type of the cross of Christ.

343. That soul which has no other aim than the perfect observance of the law of our Lord, and the carrying of the cross of Christ, will be a true ark containing the true manna, which is God.

344. If you wish devotion to be born in your heart, the love of God to grow, together with the desire for divine things, cleanse your soul from every desire and self-seeking, so that nothing of the kind remain with you. For as a sick man, freed from the evil humours which troubled him, feels instantly returning health and a taste for his food, so shall you recover your health in God if you rid yourself of your spiritual disorders : and if this be not done, whatever you may do, you will make no progress.

345. Live in this world as if God and your soul only

were in it ; that your heart may be a captive to no earthly thing.

346. Do not weary yourself to no purpose, nor seek spiritual joy and sweetness, unless it be by denying yourself in that which you aim at.

347. If you would attain to holy recollection, it must be by rejecting, and not by admitting.

348. Be interiorly detached from all things, and do not set your affection upon any temporal thing, and your soul will gather in a harvest of blessings beyond its comprehension.

349. The goods of God, which are beyond all measure, can be contained only in an empty and solitary heart.

350. So far as it lies in your power, refuse nothing asked of you, though you may have heed of it yourself.

351. He will never attain to perfection who will not labour to be satisfied with this : that all his natural and spiritual desires should be satisfied in the absence of everything which is not God. This is most necessary for abiding peace and tranquillity of spirit.

352. Let your soul be always ordered by a desire not for that which is easy, but for that which is most difficult ; not for that which is most pleasant, but for that which is most unpleasant ; not for that which is elevated and precious, but for that which is vile and despised ; not for great things, but for little things : not to seek for any-

thing, but to seek for nothing ; not for that which is best, but for that which is worst ; desiring to enter, for the love of Jesus, upon detachment, emptiness, and poverty in everything in this world.

353. If you will cleanse your soul of strange possessions and desires, you will understand all things spiritually ; and if you will restrain yourself from setting your heart upon them, you will rejoice truly in them, and understand them certainly.

354. All people will be your servants, and all things will minister to you, if only you will forget them and yourself.

355. You will never have to do with necessities greater than those to which you made your heart yield itself : for the poor in spirit are most happy and joyous in a state of privation ; and he who has set his heart upon nothing, finds fulness everywhere.

356. The poor in spirit give generously all they have, and their pleasure consists in being thus deprived of everything for God's sake, and out of love to their neighbour, ordering all things by the law of this virtue.

357. Poverty of spirit looks to the substance of devotion solely, and making use only of what is sufficient for it, is weary of the multiplicity and curiosity of visible means.

358. A soul withdrawn from exterior things, detached

from its own will, even in divine things, will not be raised by prosperity nor subdued by adversity.

359. The poor that are naked shall be clothed : and the soul that will strip itself of all its desires, likings, and dislikings, God will clothe with His own purity, His own joy, and His own will.

360. The love of God in a pure and simple soul, detached from every desire, is frequently in act.

361. Restrain your desires, and you will find that which your heart longs for : how can you tell that your desire is according to the will of God ?

362. If you desire to have your soul in peace and comfort, and to serve God in truth, do not rest satisfied with what you have done in the way of self-denial, for it may be that on the new road you have entered, you may find yourself as much hindered, or even more than you were ; but give up everything that you have.

363. If you fail in the practice of self-denial, which is the sum and root of virtue : every other way is but beating the air, and you will make no progress, notwithstanding most profound meditations and communications.

364. Not only do temporal goods, the delights and the tastes of sense, hinder and thwart the way of God, but spiritual delights and consolations also, if sought for, or clung to eagerly, disturb the way of virtue.

365. Such is the nature of our vain concupiscence that it clings to everything : like the dry-rot, which wastes away what is sound, it has its way both in what is good and what is bad.

PRAYER OF THE ENAMOURED SOUL

O Lord God, my Love, if Thou art still mindful of my sins, and wilt not grant my petitions, Thy will be done, for that is my chief desire. Show Thou Thy goodness and mercy, and Thou shalt be known by them. If it be that Thou art waiting for my good works, that in them Thou mayest grant my petition, do Thou give them and work them in me : send also the penalties which Thou wilt accept, and do Thou inflict them. But if Thou art not waiting for my good works ; what art Thou waiting for, O most merciful Lord ? why tarriest Thou ? For if at last it must be grace and mercy, for which I pray in Thy Son, do Thou accept my worthless offering, according to Thy will, and give me this good also according to Thy will. O Lord Almighty, my spirit has fainted within me because it has forgotten to feed upon Thee. I knew Thee not, O my Lord, when I went after vanity.

2. Who can free himself from base and mean ways, if Thou, O my God, wilt not lift him up to Thee in pure love ? Thou hastenest joyfully and lovingly, O Lord,

to raise up him who has offended Thee, but I make no
haste to honour and raise him up who has offended
me. How shall a man raise himself up to Thee, for
he is born and bred in misery, if Thou wilt not lift
him up with the hand that made him ? O Lord
Almighty, if the shadow of the power of Thy justice in
earthly sovereigns who govern and rule the nations can
do so much, what cannot Thy almighty justice do,
dealing with the just man and the sinner ?

3. O Lord my God, Thou art not estranged from him
who does not estrange himself from Thee. How is it
that men say Thou art absent ? O Lord my God, who
is there that seeks Thee in pure and true love, who does
not find Thee to be the joy of His will ? It is Thou who
art the first to show Thyself, going forth to meet those
who desire to meet Thee. Thou wilt not take away from
me, O my God, what Thou hast once given me in Thy
only begotten Son Jesus Christ, in Whom Thou hast
given me all I desire. I will therefore rejoice, Thou wilt
not tarry if I wait for Thee. Wait in hope then, O my
soul, for from henceforth thou mayest love God in thy
heart.

4. The heavens are mine, the earth is mine, and the
nations are mine : mine are the just, and the sinners are
mine : mine are the angels, and the Mother of God ; all
things are mine, God Himself is mine and for me, be-

cause Christ is mine, and all for me. What dost thou then ask for, what dost thou seek for, O my soul ? All is thine, all is for thee ; do not take less, nor rest with the crumbs which fall from the table of Thy Father. Go forth and exult in thy glory, hide thyself in it, and rejoice, and thou shalt obtain all the desires of thy heart.

5. O sweetest love of God, too little known ; he who has found Thee is at rest ; let everything change, O my God, that we may rest in Thee. Everywhere with Thee, O my God, everywhere all things with Thee as I wish. O my Love, all for Thee, nothing for me : nothing for Thee, everything for me. All sweetness and delight for Thee, none for me : all bitterness and trouble for me, none for Thee. O my God, how sweet to me Thy presence, who art the sovereign Good. I will draw near to Thee in silence, and will uncover Thy feet,* that it may please Thee to unite me to Thyself, making my soul Thy bride : I will rejoice in nothing till I am in Thine arms. O Lord, I beseech Thee, leave me not for a moment, because I know not the value of my soul.

* Ruth iii. 7, 9.

POEMS

POEMS

THE DARK NIGHT

1   I DEPARTED in the darkness
     With the pains of love oppressed,
     Happy lot ! for none observed me ;
     All my house was then at rest,

2   By the ladder that is secret,
     In the darkness on I pressed,
     Through the night, disguised in safety,
     All my house was then at rest.

3   Unobserved and unobserving
     In the silent blissful night ;
     And in my heart the fire burning
     Was my only guide and light.

4   To the place where He was waiting,
     Safely guided on the way
     On I went ; the light was brighter
     Than the sunshine of mid-day.

5   Night that led to my Beloved,—
     Guide and light upon the way—
     And made us one ; night more lovely
     Than the dawn of coming day.

6   On my breast with flowers covered,
     Which for Him alone I kept,
     I caressed Him ; and the cedars
     Waving fanned Him while He slept.

7 When His tresses were disordered
   By the motion of the air,
   Then I fainted, and He struck me
   With His hand so soft and fair.

8 Self-forgetting, there I rested
   On my love reclined my head,
   All anxieties discarded
   Mid the lilies round me spread.

SONG OF THE SOUL AND ITS BRIDE-GROOM

1 O MY love, where art Thou hiding?
   Why hast Thou forsaken me?
   Thou hast left me to my sorrow,
   To bewail my loss of Thee.
   Thou hast wounded me and swiftly
   As the hart hast fled away,
   I pursued Thee, crying loudly,
   Thou wert gone, and wouldest not stay.

2 O ye shepherds, I entreat you,
   As you wend your watchful way,
   To the hill, amid the sheepcots
   Every night and every day,
   Tell my love, if you shall see him,
   Of the state in which I lie,
   Of my longing, and in longing
   That I languish, pine, and die.

3 In my quest of Him no mountains,
   Nor wide plains shall me delay;
   I will never stoop to gather
   Even a flower on the way.

I will cross the frontiers boldly,
Nor shall giants hold me back,
And if savage beasts surround me
I shall dread not their attack.

4 O ye trees of trackless forests,
And ye thickets of the land ;
Shade and shelter for the weary,
Planted by his loving hand.
O ye meadows, fresh and verdant,
Pictures of the land above,
Decked with flowers bright and fragrant
Tell me, have you seen my Love ?

THE CREATURES ANSWER

5 We have seen Him ! we have seen Him !
O ! the beauty of His face !
Moving through the groves, and pouring
Down the treasures of His grace.
Hastening on, He looked upon them—
O ! that look ! how full of love —
And the groves became more lovely
With a beauty from above.

THE BRIDE

6 I am wounded ; who can heal me ?
Sorrow-laden, lone, and sad ;
Longing for Thy wonted presence,
That alone can make me glad.
Come Thyself, and do not tarry ;
Send no messengers to me ;
They are powerless to tell me
Aught that I would know of Thee.

7. All who serve Thee—men and angels—
Each in his determined place
Speak to me, with voice unceasing,
Of thy comeliness and grace.

They but make my wound still greater,
  There is that beyond my reach
And leaves me dead ; what I know not,
  For they stammer in their speech.

8 O my life, how thou persistest
    In continuing the strife,
  For by living on thou livest
    Where is not thy real life.
  All thou knowest of thy Lover
    Are as arrows in thy heart
  Sent to slay thee ; then how is it
    Thou abidest as thou art ?

9 My Beloved, Thou hast planted
    In my heart the darts of love ;
  Why dost Thou refuse to heal it
    With the unction from above ?
  Now that Thou hast robbed me of it—
    I in desolation left—
  Why hast Thou not taken it with Thee
    And thus · perfected the theft ?

10 Tribulations overwhelm me
    By anxieties oppressed ;
  Thou alone canst free me from them,
    Therefore give me peace and rest.
  Let mine eyes then look upon Thee,
    For it is by Thee they see ;
  They are Thine, and Thou hast made them,
    I will keep them all for Thee.

11 O that Thou the clouds would'st scatter
    That between us darkly lie,
  Show Thy face, and in the beauty
    Of the vision let me die.
  For the beatific vision
    That makes glad the saints above,
  Is the only perfect healing
    Of the malady of love.

12 Crystal spring of limpid waters
    Unexhausted in its flow ;
    O that on thy silvered surface,
    As a mirror, Thou would'st show
    Unto me those eyes so lovely,
    And which I so long to see,
    For their image is already
    Outlined on my heart from Thee.

13 My Beloved, look not at me
    With those eyes so full of love ;
    I am flying, overpowered.

THE BRIDEGROOM

    O return to me, my dove ;
    On the hill the hart is looming,
    And the arrow to it clings
    In the air refreshed that stirreth
    By the motion of thy wings.

THE BRIDE

14 My Beloved is the mountains—
    They reveal Him unto me—
    And the lonely wooded valleys
    With the islands of the sea,
    Strange and lovely ; and the murmur
    Of the waters as they flow,
    And the sweet entrancing whisper
    Of the winds that softly blow.

15 My Beloved is the silent
    Tranquil night before the morn ;
    Ere the ruddy dawn approaches
    And another day is born.
    He is music that is soundless ;
    In the wilderness a voice,
    And the supper that refresheth
    Making hearts that love rejoice.

17

16   Who will catch for us the foxes
        That so cunningly repair
     To the vineyard Thou hast planted,
        Now so fruitful and so fair ?
     While we move among the flowers
        And our hands with roses' fill,
     For the making of a garland
        Let none appear on the hill.

17   Chilling north wind, from thy caverns
        Send no more the blasts that kill ;
     Come thou south wind, love enkindling,
        And the air with odours fill.
     There among the fragrant flowers
        My Beloved will abide,
     And will feed among the lilies
        In the garden of His bride.

18   Now the rose trees and the flowers
        Bloom and blossom in their beds,
     And around the fragrant amber
        Its delicious perfume sheds.
     Nymphs of Juda come not nigh us,
        In the suburbs still remain ;
     That ye may not touch the threshold
        Of our house, your feet restrain.

19   Hide Thyself, then, my Beloved,
        And let none Thy presence trace,
     Keep for me alone the secret ;
        To the mountains turn Thy face ;
     But with loving eyes regarding,
        Look on those who wait on me
     On my way among the islands
        Of a strange and stormy sea.

THE BRIDEGROOM

20 Cruel lions of the forest,
   Crouching in their secret lair ;
Fawns and does so wild and restless,
   And all the birds of the air.
Nightly terrors that alarm us,
   Gloomy valleys, lowly plain,
Burning heat and lofty mountains,
   Howling winds and driving rain.

21 By the music of the viols,
   By the siren's soothing strain,
I adjure you and command you
   From your fury to refrain.
Cease your clamours, come not nigh us,
   At a distance still abide,
And occasion no disturbance
   Of the slumbers of the bride.

22 Now the garden sheds its perfume,
   For the winter's cold is past,
And the bride in all her beauty
   Has come into it at last.
There, content among the lilies,
   In the everlasting arms,
She is tranquilly reposing,
   Henceforth free from all alarms.

23 When I saw thee wan and weary,
   Underneath the apple tree ;
I held out My hand in pity,
   And betrothed Me unto thee.
When thy mother deluded fell,
   In the snare the traitor laid,
There the price of thy redemption,
   In My bitter death was paid.

THE BRIDE

24 Dens of lions are the fences
      That protect the bridal bed
    Hung with purple : fragrant flowers
      All around their perfume shed.
    It was wrought in peace and quiet,
      Who will touch it ? None so bold,
    For its manifold adornments
      Are a thousand shields of gold.

25 They are running in Thy footsteps,
      On the road which Thou didst tread
    In the odour of the ointment
      That was poured upon Thy head.
    The burning fire now has touched them
      And the inner furnace glows ;
    And the strengthening wine is tasted,
      While the heavenly balsam flows.

26 My Beloved gently led me
      By the hand, O love divine !
    Placed me in the inner cellar
      Where I drank the wondrous wine.
    Coming forth I wandered lonely
      O'er the plain, and knew no more,
    Having lost the flock I followed
      In the days that went before.

27 He embraced me there and taught me
      Sitting humbly at His feet,
    Wondrous secrets of His wisdom :
      And the learning is so sweet.
    There I also made a promise
      I would be His faithful bride,
    True and constant ; by that promise
      I will stedfastly abide.

28 My Beloved is my Bridegroom
        And my Lord—O what a joy !
    I will henceforth all the powers
        Of my soul for Him employ.
    And the flock that once I tended,
        Now I tend not as before,
    For my only occupation
        Is to love Him more and more.

29 I have gone away for ever
        From the haunts of idle men,
    And a sharer in their follies
        I will never be again.
    They may say, and say it loudly,
        I am lost ; but I am not ;
    I was found by my Beloved,
        O how blessed is my lot !

30 We will go in early morning
        While the dew is on the ground,
    To the garden where the flowers
        In their beauty may be found ;
    And will make a garland of them
        In which emeralds shall shine
    Knit and bound and held together
        By a single hair of mine.

31 By that single hair that fluttered
        On my neck and seen by Thee—
    Thou did'st look again upon it
        . And wert by it drawn to me.
    Thou wert made a willing captive,
        Weak and slender though it be,
    And I dared to look upon Thee,
        And in looking wounded Thee.

32 While on me Thine eyes were resting,
        Full of sweet and gracious love,
    They impressed on me their beauty ;
        Heavenly beauty from above.

Then Thy love flowed in upon me
And mine eyes obtained the grace
What they saw in Thee to worship,
O the beauty of Thy face.

33 I was once unclean and swarthy,
In a miserable plight;
Yet I pray Thee not to spurn me,
Or to cast me from Thy sight.
Of my former degradation,
There remaineth not a trace,
For Thine eyes have rested on me,
Shedding comeliness and grace.

THE BRIDEGROOM

34 The little dove, white and stainless,
Wings her way, returning now,
To the ark of safety, bearing
In her mouth the olive bough.
Now her melancholy cooings
Will the turtle dove abate,
On the verdant banks rejoicing
In the presence of her mate.

35 Now the little dove was living
In her solitude at rest;
For in solitude, contented,
She had built herself her nest.
The Beloved had been leading
Into solitude the dove,   ·
And in solitude was wounded
With the arrows of her love.

THE BRIDE

36 In our common love rejoicing,
My Beloved, let us go
To the summit of the mountain
Whence the limpid waters flow.

To the hill of contemplation,
There each other to behold
In Thy beauty :—Let us enter
Into mysteries untold.

37 We will go at once together,
My Beloved and His bride,
To the dark and secret caverns
Of the rock, and there to hide.
Into those mysterious caverns
Where no earthly light can shine,
We will enter—there in secret
We will taste the heavenly wine.

38 For within those secret caverns
Thou Thyself wilt shew to me,
That which I am always longing
In my inmost heart to see.
In the innermost recesses
Of the caverns Thou wilt give,
What the other day Thou gavest,
O my life ; in Thee I live.

39 I shall breathe the air that quickeneth,
And the nightingale shall sing ;
In my raptured ear, the music
Of her voice shall sweetly ring ;
Pleasant grove and all its beauty,
With the marvels it contains,
In the night ; with the fire burning
That consumes and never pains.

40 I went in with my Beloved,
Seen by no created eye,
Nor with all his strength and cunning
Durst Aminadabad come nigh.
Then the siege was intermitted,
Then abandoned by the foe ;
And the cavalry dismounted
When it saw the waters flow.

THE LIVING FLAME OF LOVE

1 O LIVING flame of love,
      How painless is the smart,
   Thy tender wounds create
      Within my very heart ;
   Oh end at last the weary strife
   And break the web of this my life.

2 O gentle hand and touch,
      O wound in sweetness rife,
   O burning, a foretaste
      Of everlasting life.
   The debt is paid that long was due,
   And death by death brings life anew.

3 O lamps of fire that burn,
      Illumining the night,
   Sense in its caverns glows
      With unaccustomed light.
   They once were dark but now are bright,
   And to my Love give warmth and light.

4 How loving Thou dost lie
      Awake within my breast,
   And by Thyself alone,
      In secret there at rest.
   The sweetness of Thy blissful breath
   Makes strong my love ; and strong as death.

A SOUL LONGING FOR THE VISION OF GOD

   I LIVE, and yet not I,
   In a manner hoping
   That I am dying because I am not dead.

I

I am not now living in myself,
And without God I cannot live ;
For without Him, I am also without myself.
This life of mine, what is it ?
A thousand deaths to me ;
For I am waiting for my very life,
Dying because I am not dead.

II

This life that I am living
Is a lifeless life.
And so a death continuing,
Until I come to live with Thee.
O God, hear Thou my cry !
This life of mine I will it not ;
I die because I am not dead.

III

When I am away from Thee,
What is my life to me ?
The agony of death.
None greater have I ever seen.
O, wretched that I am !
For while I am living on
I die because I am not dead.

IV

The fish that from the water leapeth
Is not without relief ;
The death that it endures
Does end in death at last.
What death can ever equal
My misery of life ?
For I, the more I live, the more I die.

V

When I see Thee in the Sacrament
And begin to be relieved,
The absence of fruition
Creates a deeper pang ;
All brings greater pain,
And the pain is so bitter
That I am dying because I am not dead.

VI

And if, O Lord, I have a joy
In the hope of seeing Thee ;
My sorrow is increased,
Because I fear to lose Thee.
Living in dread so great
And hoping as I hope,
I die, because I am not dead.

VII

From this death deliver me,
O God, and give me life,
Nor let these fetters hold me ;
They are so strong :
Behold, I die to see Thee,
And in a manner hoping
That I am dying, because I am not dead.

VIII

My death I will bewail then,
And lament my life
By reason of my sins
Still here prolonged.
O my God, when shall I be there
Where I may truly say,
I live at last because I am not dead ?

ECSTASY OF CONTEMPLATION

I ENTERED, but I knew not where,
And there I stood nought knowing,
All science transcending.

I

I knew not where I entered,
For, when I stood within,
Not knowing where I was,
I heard great things.
What I heard I will not tell :
I was there as one who knew not,
All science transcending.

II

Of peace and devotion
The knowledge was perfect,
In solitude profound ;
The right way was clear,
But so secret was it,
That I stood babbling,
All science transcending.

III

I stood enraptured
In ecstasy, beside myself,
And in my every sense
No sense remained.
My spirit was endowed
With understanding, understanding nought,
All science transcending.

IV

The higher I ascended
The less I understood.
It is the dark cloud
Illumining the night.

Therefore, he who understands,
Knows nothing ever
All science transcending.

V

He who really ascends so high
Annihilates himself,
And all his previous knowledge
Seems ever less and less ;
His knowledge so increases
That he knoweth nothing,
All science transcending.

VI

This knowing that knows nothing
Is so potent in its might
That the prudent in their reasoning
Never can defeat it ;
For their wisdom never reaches
To the understanding that understandeth nothing,
All science transcending.

VII

This sovereign wisdom
Is of an excellence so high
That no faculty nor science
Can ever unto it attain.
He who shall overcome himself
By the knowledge which knows nothing,
Will always rise all science transcending.

VIII

And if you would listen ;
This sovereign wisdom doth consist
In a sense profound
Of the essence of God :
It is an act of His compassion,
To leave us, nought understanding,
All science transcending.

THE SAME SUBJECT

I

In an act of daring love,
And not of hope abandoned,
I mounted higher and higher,
So that I came in sight of the prey.

II

That I might come in sight
Of that prey divine,
I was forced to fly so high
As to be lost to sight ;
Yet in that act supreme
I grew weaker in my flight,
But my love was still so strong
That I came in sight of the prey.

III

When I ascended higher
My sight grew faint and dim,
And my greatest conquest
Was in the darkness made ;
But as my love was strong
Blindly forth I leapt,
I mounted higher and higher,
So that I came in sight of the prey.

IV

In a way most strange
I made a thousand flights in one,
For the hope that is from heaven,
What it hopes, attains ;
This was my only hope
And my hope was not in vain,
For I mounted higher and higher,
So that I came in sight of the prey.

V

But the nearer I drew
In this act sublime,
The more lowly, base, and vile,
And humiliated I grew.
I said, none can reach it ;
And abasing myself more and more ;
I mounted higher and higher,
So that I came in sight of the prey.

GOD THE SUPREME GOOD

WITHOUT support, and with support,
Without light and in darkness living,
I see myself wasting away.

I

My soul is detached
From every thing created,
And raised above itself
Into a life delicious,
Of God alone supported.
And therefore I will say,
That what I most esteem
Is that my soul is now
Without support, and with support.

II

And though I am in darkness,
In this mortal life
My misery is not so great :
For if I have not light
I have the life celestial ;
For the love of that life,
In the excess of its blindness,
Keeps the soul submissive,
Without light and in darkness living.

III

Love is doing this ;
I have known it since,
For be it ill or well with me
It makes all one joy.
It transforms my soul ;
And so in its sweet flame,
Which in myself I feel,
I see myself rapidly burning
And wasting away.

THE SAME SUBJECT

For all the beauty of the world
Never will I lose myself,
But only for that I know not,
Which happily is found.

I

Sweetness of good that is finite,
The utmost it can do
Is to pall upon the appetite
And vitiate the taste.
For all the sweetness in the world
Never will I lose myself,
But only for that I know not,
Which happily is found.

II

The generous heart
Will never rest
Where it can be at ease,
But only where it meets with difficulties
Nought can ever satisfy it ;
And its faith ascends so high
As to taste of that I know not,
Which happily is found.

III

He that is on fire with love
Divinely touched of God
Receives a taste so new
That all his own is gone.
Like one who of a fever ill
Loathes the food before him,
And longs for that I know not,
Which happily is found.

IV

Be not at this astonished,
That the taste should thus be changed ;
For the cause of this affection
From all others differs.
And so every thing created
Is an alien to it ;
And it tastes that I know not,
Which happily is found.

V

For when once the will
Has been touched of God,
It never can be satisfied
Except in God alone.
But because His beauty
Is such that faith alone can see it,
It tastes it in I know not what,
Which happily is found.

VI

And now of Him enamoured,
Tell me if you are in pain ;
For there is no sweetness
In any thing created.
Alone without form and figure,
Without support or rest,
Tasting there I know not what,
Which happily is found.

VII

Do not think the inner heart,
Which is of priceless worth,
Rejoices or is glad
In that which here sweetness gives ;
But rather above all beauty raised
That is, can be, or has ever been,
Tastes there I know not what,
Which happily is found.

VIII

He who seeks a greater gain
Will rather turn his thoughts
To that he has not acquired
Than to that he has already.
And therefore for a greater venture
I shall always be inclined,
Neglecting all for that I know not,
Which happily is found.

IX

For all that in the way of sense
I may obtain on earth,
And all I may understand,
However high it may be—
For all grace and beauty—
Never will I lose myself ;
But only for that I know not,
Which happily is found.

SONG OF THE SOUL REJOICING IN THE KNOWLEDGE OF GOD BY FAITH

I KNOW the fountain well which flows and runs,
Though it be night.

18

I

That everlasting fountain is a fountain hid,
And where it is I know well,
    Though it be night.

II

Its source I know not, because it has none ;
But I know that therein all things begin,
    Though it be night.

III

I know that nothing can be in beauty like it,
And that of it heaven and earth do drink,
    Though it be night.

IV

I know well it is of depths unfathomable,
And that none can ever sound it,
    Though it be night.

V

Its brightness is never dimmed,
And I know that from it all light proceeds,
    Though it be night.

VI

I know its streams are so abundant,
It waters hell and heaven and earth,
    Though it be night.

VII

The torrent that from this fountain rises,
I know well is so grand and so strong,
    Though it be night.

This everlasting fountain lies concealed
In the living Bread to give us life,
    Though it be night.

IX

It calls on every creature to be filled
With its waters, but in the dark,
    Though it be night.

X

This living fountain for which I long
I see in this Bread of life, I see it now,
    Though it be night.

SONG OF CHRIST AND THE SOUL

I

A SHEPHERD is alone and in pain,
Deprived of all pleasure and joy,
His thoughts on his shepherdess intent,
And his heart is by love most cruelly torn.

II

He weeps, not because he is wounded with love,
And his distress brings him no pain,
Though a wound is made in his heart;
But he weeps because he thinks he is forgot.

III

His beautiful shepherdess, so does he think,
Has forgotten him : that thought alone
Makes him suffer in the land of the stranger,
And his heart is by love most cruelly torn.

IV

The shepherd exclaims, Ah wretch that I am!
For I am abandoned and left;
My presence is shunned by my love,
And my heart for her love is most cruelly torn.

V

At last he was raised on a tree,
Where he opened his beautiful arms,
And on it, he died,
His heart by love most cruelly torn.

THE MOST HOLY TRINITY *

(In principio erat Verbum).

I

IN the beginning was the Word,
The Word was God,
In Whom He possessed
Bliss everlasting.

II

The Word was God,
He is the Beginning;
He was in the Beginning,
And never began.

III

He was the Beginning itself,
And therefore had none;
The Word is the Son,
From the beginning born.

* Composed while in prison at Toledo, 1578. (*See* Relation of
Maria del Sacramento, *Escritoras españolas*, ii. 176.)

IV

He has begotten for ever,
And is for ever begetting ;
He gives Him of His substance for ever,
And has it for ever Himself.

V

And thus the glory of the Son
Is that He hath in the Father,
And all His glory the Father
Hath in the Son.

VI

As the lover with his love,
Each in the other living,
So this Love which Both unites
Is One in Both.

VII

In dignity and might
Coequal with them Both,
Three Persons, and one Love,
The Three are One.

VIII

And in the Three one Love,
One Lover makes of All ;
The Lover is the Love
In Whom Each doth live.

IX

The Being which the Three possess
Each by Himself possesses,
And of the three Each loves the other
In that He hath this Being.

X

This Being is Each One,
And alone makes Them One
In a way ineffable,
Beyond the reach of words.

XI

And so that Love which makes Them One
Is Infinite Itself ;
For one Love make One the Three,
And is their Being as well,
And that Love the more it makes Them One
The more It is Their Love.

THE COMMUNICATION OF THE THREE PERSONS

I

IN the Love from Both proceeding
It hath limits none.
Words of gladness spoke the Father
To His only Son.

II

Words they were of joy profoundest,
Understood of none,
But of Him exulting in them,
Whose they were—the Son.

III

Of these words of gladness, only
This was heard by me—
Nought, my Son, can give Me pleasure
When I have not Thee.

IV

But if aught should give Me pleasure,
  That I seek in Thee,
He who gives to Thee most pleasure
  Gives it most to Me.

V

He who Thee in nought resembleth
  Cannot be like Me.
Life of Life, My whole rejoicing
  Is alone in Thee.

VI

Thou art My Eternal Wisdom,
  Thou, Light of My light;
In Thee, Figure of My substance,
  Is my whole delight.

VII

Thee, My Son, he who loveth
  Shall have love of Me
And the love wherewith I love him
  Is My love of Thee.
So great, then, is My love of Thee, that he
Who loveth Thee shall be also loved by Me.

THE CREATION

I

O MY Son, I long to give Thee
  In my love a loving bride,
Who shall by Thy goodness merit
  With Us ever to abide:

II

Who shall, at the heavenly banquet,
  Eating of My bread with Me,
Learn to know the wondrous treasure,
  That I have, My Son, in Thee ;

III

And that in Thy grace and beauty,
  As a glory round her shed,
She with Me may joy together.
  Then the Son gave thanks and said :—

IV

On the bride which Thou wilt give Me
  I My brightness will bestow,
So that she My Father's goodness
  In its light may love and know ;
Learning also how My Being
  From His being doth overflow.

V

With My arms I will embrace her
  And Thy love shall be her light,
So for ever shall Thy goodness
  Be exalted with delight.

THE SAME SUBJECT

I

For the merits of Thy love, then,
  ' Be it done,' the Father said ;
In the word the Father uttered
  All created things were .made.

II

In the everlasting wisdom
  Rose the palace of the bride,
Which two substances created
  In a twofold form divide.

III

With varieties unnumbered
  Was the lower part arrayed,
While the higher glowed in beauty,
  With the wondrous gems displayed.

IV

That the bride might know the Bridegroom
  Who her heavenly nuptials graced,
The Angelic hosts in order
  In the higher part were placed.

V

Man was placed—his nature lower—
  In the lower part on earth,
Being fashioned of a substance
  Which was of inferior worth.

VI

And although both place and nature
  God in this way did divide,
Yet the two are, both together,
  But one body of the bride.

VII

And the two, although divided,
  Are one bride in His one love,
Who, in gladness, as the Bridegroom
  Is possessed by those above.

VIII

Those below in hope are living
Of the faith that He has given,
For one day He will exalt them—
He hath said so—unto heaven.

IX

For of those of base condition
He will take away the shame,
And exalt them, so that nothing
Shall remain to them of blame.

X

He in all things with their likeness
Will Himself one day invest ;
He will come and dwell among them,
As His own elected rest.

XI

God Himself will be incarnate,
God will have a human birth ;
Eating, He will come, and drinking,
And converse with men on earth.

XII

He will dwell Himself among them
And continually stay,
Till the final consummation—
When the ages melt away.

XIII

Then shall both rejoice together
In an endless life of bliss,
For to Him belongs the headship
Of the bride, and she is His.

XIV

He shall bring the just together—
Nought shall them from her divide—
For they are the living members
Of the body of the bride.

XV

He will tenderly embrace her,
He will give her of His love,
And, united with Him, take her,
To His Father's home above.

XV

Into joy shall she then enter :
God no greater joy can give ;
When absorbed in Him for ever
She the life of God shall live.

XVII

So the Father, Son, and Spirit,
Three in One and One in Three,
Live, Each living in the Other,
The most blessed Trinity.

THE DESIRES OF THE HOLY FATHERS *

I

WHEN the ancient saints were waiting,
Hope came down to their relief,
And made lighter by its presence
The sore pressure of their grief.

* *Rorate coeli desuper et nubes pluant Justum.*—Is. xlv. 8.

II

But still, hope deferred, together
  With the longing which they had
To behold the promised Bridegroom,
  Made them sick at heart, and sad.

III

Pouring forth their supplications—
  In their misery they lay,
Sighing, weeping, and lamenting,
  With strong crying night and day,—

IV

That He would the times determine,
  And among them come and stay ;
' O that I,' so one entreated,
  ' Might rejoice to see His day ! '

V

' Hasten, then, Thy work, and finish ;
  Send Him, Lord, Whom Thou wilt send,'
Was the cry of one. Another's,
  ' O that He the heavens would rend !

VI

' That I might behold His coming,
  And my wail be turned to mirth ;
Let the clouds rain down the Just one,
  So long desired on the earth ;

VII

' Let the earth which brought forth briers
  Now break forth, and in their room
Let it bear the sacred flower
  Which shall ever on it bloom.'

VIII

Others also : ' O how blessed
Shall that generation be !
Which shall merit in time coming
God's Most Holy Face to see ; '

IX

' Men shall throng around, and touch, Him,
They shall in His sight remain ;
In the sacraments rejoicing
He Himself shall then ordain.'

THE SAME SUBJECT

I

THESE and other supplications,
As the centuries rolled by,
Men poured forth : with greater fervour
As the promised time drew nigh.

II

Aged Simeon in the furnace
Of his longing, burning lay,
Praying God that He would grant him
Of His grace to see that day.

III

And the Ever-blessed Spirit
Condescended to his cry ;
And consoled him with the promise
That the old man should not die

IV

Till he saw the Ever-living
God, descending from above,
Took Him in his arms and held Him,
And embraced Him in His love.

THE INCARNATION

I

In the fulness of the ages
Now had come the holy tide,
For the payment of the ransom
Of the long-expectant bride,

II

Groaning in the house of bondage
Underneath the legal yoke
Of the precepts given by Moses,
When these words the Father spoke :

III

' I, my Son, have in Thy likeness
And Thy image made Thy bride,
And in that resemblance worthy
To be ever at Thy side ;

IV

' But in one respect unlike Thee,
For her nature is not Thine :
She is flesh—her nature human—
While Thy nature is divine.

V

' Perfect love demands a likeness
In the lovers it unites,
For the most complete resemblance
Most aboundeth in delights.

VI

' Now the love and exultation
Of the bride would greatly grow
If she saw Thee in her likeness,
In the flesh, on earth below.'

VII

Then the Son the Father answered:
' Lo ! My will is ever Thine,
And my glory which I cherish
 Is that Thine is also Mine.

VIII

' I am ready at Thy bidding,
 For Thy will is my delight,
To make known at once Thy goodness
And Thy wisdom and Thy might.

IX

' I will manifest Thy justice,
 And proclaim throughout the earth
Thy supremacy and beauty
 And the sweetness of Thy worth.

X

' I will go and seek My bride, then,
 And upon Myself will take
All the poverty and sorrows
 She now suffers for my sake.

XI

' And that I true life may give her,
 I will give for her My own,
So shall I present her, rescued,
 From the pit, before Thy throne.'

THE SAME SUBJECT

I

GOD then summoned the archangel
 Holy Gabriel—him He sent
To the Blessed Virgin Mary
 To obtain the maid's consent.

II

She consented : in that instant
  The mysterious work was done,
And the Trinity a body
  Wrought and fashioned for the Son.

III

In this wondrous operation,
  Though the Sacred Three concurred,
He who in the womb of Mary
  Was incarnate, is the Word.

IV

He Who had a Father only
  Had a Mother also then :
But it was in other fashion
  Than the manner is of men.

V

In the womb of Holy Mary
  He His flesh did then receive :
So the Son of God Most Highest
  We the Son of Man believe.

THE NATIVITY

I

Now at last the destined ages
  Their appointed course had run,
When rejoicing from His chamber
  Issued forth the Bridegroom Son.

II

He embraced His bride, and held her
  Lovingly upon His breast,
And the gracious Mother laid Him
  In the manger down to rest.

III

There He lay, the dumb beasts by Him,
They were fitly stabled there,
While the shepherds and the angels
Filled with melody the air.

IV

So the feast of their espousals
With solemnity was kept ;
But Almighty God, an infant ;
In the manger moaned and wept.

V

So the bride at her betrothal
Did the bridal gifts arrange ;
But the Mother looked in wonder
At the marvellous exchange.

VI

Man gave forth a song of gladness,
God Himself a plaintive moan ;
Both possessing that which never
Had been hitherto their own.

SUPER FLUMINA BABYLONIS *

(Ps. cxxxvi.)

I

By the waters of the river—
Close by Babylon it swept—
On the banks—my tears were flowing—
There I set me down and wept.

II

I remembered thee, O Sion,
With thy love my heart was sore ;
Sweet to me was thy memorial,
So I wept still more and more,

* Composed while in prison at Toledo, 1578.

III

Of my festal robes divested,
  Those of woe around me flung,
While my silent harp suspended
  From the willow branches hung.

IV

There I left it; fondly trusting,
  For my hopes in thee still lay.
Love my heart had deeply wounded,
  And had carried it away.

V

So, I said, my wound is grievous;
  O let love me wholly slay.
Into its fires then I threw me,
  That I might be burned away.

VI

Now the silly moth I blame not,
  That in the fire seeks its death;
For I, while in myself but dying,
  Draw in thee alone my breath.

VII

I for thee to death submitted,
  And for thee to life returned;
For in thy most sweet memorial
  Life and death were both inurned.

VIII

In their merriment exulting,
  Heedless of their captive's wrongs,
Strangers bade me rise and sing them
  Sion's old familiar songs.

IX

Sing us of the songs of Sion ;
We would hear them—strange demand—
How can I, lamenting Sion,
Sing them in a foreign land ?

X

In the chants once so familiar
How can I uplift my voice ?
May they never be remembered
If in exile I rejoice !

XI

Let my tongue from speech refraining,
To my palate silent cleave ;
If I, in the land of exile.
Where I dwell alone and grieve,

XII

Even amidst the verdant bowers
Of the Babylonic land
Should forget thee. Let my right hand
Cease its cunning to command

XIII

If I make not thee, O Sion,
The beginning of my mirth ;
Or if I rejoice in keeping
Any festival of earth.

XIV

Thou, of Babylon the daughter,
Shalt lie prostrate in the dust,
Lost and wretched : but for ever
Blest is He in Whom I trust.

XV

In the day of retribution
    He will thee at last afflict ;
He will lay on thee the burden
    Thou didst once on me inflict,

XVI

He will me, thy weeping captive,
    With thy little children take,
And to Christ the Rock will bring them—
    I have left thee for His sake.

SONG I

SI DE MI BAJA SUERTE

The Soul's Craving

I

IF in my lowly state
The flames of love had power
    To swallow death,
And should they so increase
As to scorch up the waters of the sea—

II

And hence ascending,
Should set afire the triple elements,
    And in its flames consuming them
Should make of them its fuel—
If all these flames were love,

III

I do not think that I—
Who feel such living thirst for love—
    Could love as I desire !
Nor could the flames I number
But for a moment quench my longing.

IV

For they, compared
With that eternal and transcendent fire,
Are of no more import
Than is an atom to the whole world's bulk,
Or than a drop of water to the ocean !

V

My heart of miry clay
Hath neither heat, nor more stability
Than hath the flowering grass
Which in the hour it blooms
Is battered by the winds and droops decayed.

VI

For never could
Its fiery blaze ignite
My heart as it desires
That it might reach the heights
Of that eternal Father of all lights.

VII

O wretched fate
Which gives to love wings so inadequate !
Not only do they fail to compass
Flight that is so sublime
As doth that love supreme deserve they should do,

VIII

But I perceive, alas!
The powers of my love are so curtailed
That in its feebleness,
With wings close clipped
I hardly reach to see God in the distance.

IX

Yet, if from my base sort
These flames of love could raise me,
Until I reached to gaze on Him,
And brought me to His presence,
So that my God should look upon them—

X

Oh ! by His fire eternal
Would they be caught, with force unspeakable,
At once absorbed,
Absorbed and swallowed up
And into everlasting flame converted.

XI

Wherein my flames being drawn
Into His flames converted
Consuming in His love,
Mine own flames burnt
Would become one with His most ardent love.

XII

Thus would be realised,
At length the deepest yearning of my breast,
Seeing myself at length made one with Him
With closest tie and wholly satisfied !

Song II

MI DIOS Y MI SEÑOR, TENED MEMORIA

The Exiled Soul

I

My God, my Lord, do Thou remember
That I by faith have gazed upon Thy Face—
Lacking which sight no bliss exists for me !

II

For since I saw Thee, live I in such sort
That there is naught can bring
Joy to my soul but for an hour, or moment !

III

God of my life ! nothing can make me glad,
For all my gladness springs from sight of Thee,
And faileth me because I have Thee not.

IV

If 'tis Thy will, my God, I live forlorn,
I'll take my longings even for my comfort
While dwelling in this world.

V

With me no happiness in aught shall bide
Except the hope of seeing Thee, my God,
Where I shall never dread to lose Thee more.

VI

When shall there dawn that most delicious day
When, O my Glory, I may joy in Thee,
Delivered from this body's heavy load ?

VII

There will my bliss be measureless, entire,
At witnessing how glorious Thou art,
Wherein will lie the rapture of my life.

VIII

What will it be when I shall dwell with Thee,
Since suffering doth bring such happiness ?
Upraise me, now, O Lord, into Thy heaven !

IX

Yet if my life can bring increase of glory
To thine eternal Being,
In truth I do not wish that it should end.

X

The unending moment of the bliss of heaven
Will end my pain and anguish
So that I shall remember them no more.

XI

I went astray because I served Thee not,
As I have gained by knowing Thee, my God!
Henceforth I crave to love Thee ever more!

Song III

DECID CIELOS Y TERRA, DECID MARES

Desolation

I

TELL me, heaven, tell me, earth and ocean,
Say ye, mountains, valleys, little hillocks,
Tell me, vineyards, olive trees, and wheatfields,
Tell me, O ye plants and flowers and meadows,
    Answer, where is He
Who gave to you your beauty and your being?

II

Angels, ye who joy to look upon Him,
Blessèd souls who love Him and possess Him,
Brides, who are desirous of the Bridegroom,
Striving to obtain His sweet caresses—
    Tell me, where is He
Who gave to you your beauty and your being?

III

Ah! no answer cometh—all is silence!
Lord, when Thou speakest not, all else is mute!
My soul doth vainly seek for Thee within it,
My heart is empty, and of all bereft.

IV

Ah ! woe is me ! if war should wage within me
Whom should I find to guard me ? whom to shield ?
Joy of my soul and Glory of my spirit,
If Thóu wert absent, should I victor be ?

V

Tell me where Thou dost wander, O my Bridegroom,
Leaving in solitude the heart that loves Thee !
Where are Thy shining rays, Thou Sun resplendent,
Why hidest Thou Thy beams ?

VI

With anxious care Thou followest the sinner—
Why give no answer to the one who loves Thee ?
Why dost Thou hide Thy face, Thou Friend most cherished,
Holding me for Thine enemy ?

VII

Wherefore didst Thou depart in silence, leaving me
With no farewell ?
Be moved, Thou gentle Love, by the sad sighs
Of anguish, which break forth for Thy return.

VIII

Return to me, or bid me follow Thee,
Or bid me die ;
But force me not to live while lacking life ;
For sooth, I live not till I see Thee come.

IX

If Thou dost dwell enskied,
Let me have wings that I may fly to Thee
If in pure souls Thou find'st Thy resting place
Why dost not purify this poor polluted heart ?

X

If Thou dost make Thy home within Thy creatures,
Reveal in which of them Thou dost repose !
Where is Thy habitation, tender Lover ?
The world, without Thee, holds no place for me!

XI

O ye birds, who warble forth sweet carols,
Serpents, animals, and scaly fish,
Tell me, an ye know, tell me, where is He
Who gave to you your beauty and your being ?

THE DARK NIGHT

Aquella niebla escura

I

THIS cloud of darkness
Is light divine, strong, beautiful,
Pure, inaccessible,
Delightful, intimate,
Being the sight of God and Him alone.

II

Which to enjoy
Reaches the soul, with love all set afire ;
Becoming blind,
Beholding naught,
The essence is transcended and attained.

III

When victory is won
Over the kingdom that was held by self,
She setteth forth unseen
By all, by all unnoticed,
Searching to find her God, by Him inflamed.

IV

In this departure
The soul goes out from self and takes her flight.
Seeking her life,
She rises to th' empyreal heaven,
Casting the veil from off her secret depths.

V

Though sallying forth
Incited by the mastery of her love,
Yet in herself she holds Him—
Being engaged
In joying o'er her Good, to Him united.

VI

She rests in peace.
All images have disappeared
The intellect grown blind
The passions quelled,
The powers perforce suspended.

VII

Her glory and her bliss
Were duly reached by stairs
In safety scaled ;
Divine the way,
Formed by Christ's Mysteries.

VIII

Now having reached
The longed-for end,
Resting in her Beloved, she holds
A ceaseless motion,
Being at peace and fully satisfied.

IX

That night serene
In which her life and depths enjoy her God,
    Freed from all pain,
She searches long and ardently within herself
And with desire goes forth to meet Him.

X

    Love leads the way
Throughout the dense, dark cloud
And with no other teacher
    She safely journeys
To where God doth reveal to her His beauty.

XI

On her trackless path,
Bereft of intellect and memory,
    The King divine
Doth manifest His might and glory,
As far as may be in this mortal life.

XII

O crystal night !
Led by thy lovely glamour,
    In union divine,
The Bridegroom and the bride
Are now but one:

XIII

    While the soul
Rejoices over the eternal Word,
    A gentle wind,
Stirred by God's Holy Spirit,
Delights her very centre.

XIV

Alone they joy together
In a fair meadow by a wall enclosed,
While fragrant odours scent
    The air serene,
Making it like no other earthly spot.

XV

The King in Whom she lives
In puissant power hath robbed her of herself.
    Receiving her
As inmate of His palace,
Holds her bereft entirely of herself.

XVI

So great the strength
And force of Him to Whom she is united,—
    So weak is she,—
That yielding up herself to Him, she loses
Her own existence, being one with Him !

OH SWEET DARK NIGHT

' *Oh dulce noche escura !* '

I

O SWEET dark night
Which brings no gloomy shades,
But rather, thine obscurity
The more it blinds, the more delights the soul,
And grows in beauty as it grows more dense.

II

Divine privations,
Blest darkness, pleasant rest,
And secret inspirations !
Happy the soul made blind
By such refulgence—fortunate exchange !

III

Denying self
That it may not deny the One· Who ne'er denies.
It enters the delicious gulf
Of that blind night,
Where they who enter find a vivid light.

IV

In the hidden depths
Of this resplendent darkness,
Illumined by the Sun
Which dwelleth in her,
Night is made radiant day !

V

O night of happiness
Which offers joy in such security
To the enamoured soul,
That she in slumber rests,
And day seems night to her !

VI

To reach this rest
She mounted by the secret, hidden stairs.
When in unconsciousness,
She on their summit slept,
The rays of life fell on her.

VII

That ladder of repose,
The beauteous Mysteries of Christ,
That lovely path,
Trod by His well-loved sons,
Wherein a thousand treasures are discovered !

VIII

She soars aloft
By flight,
Having two lovely wings,
Yet, once arrived,
Their delicate plumes are scorched.

IX

There she in peace enjoys
The secret rays that stream from the 'Belovèd;
And all her house and its inhabitants
Are fallen asleep,
Powerless and free from care.

X

In drowsy rest
The dwellers in her mansions leave her free;
The Bridegroom opes and enters—
Yet when they are aroused
They murmur at their quick awakening.

XI

They enjoy His favours
In solitude, beholding not the Spouse,
For still these dwellers
Are lost in slumber
Nor do they make the slightest sound.

XII

Then the gentle bride,
Transformed and turned to her Belovèd,
Lives and reposes in Him
And draws from Him her life,
Since her own life has been consumed

XIII

While in this state
Has she repose, joy, life, and nourishment;
But on returning
To her former life,
She weeps because death lingers on its way.

XIV

Yet having wept,
Her graces still augmenting with her tears,
Her trials no longer grieve her,
For on suffering
She centres all her aims and all her love.

XV

Light in darkness;
And darkness which withdraws not in the light;
Distinctness in the mist!
The mist is manifest in light
In this abyss, and is not swallowed up.

XVI

For shade is set
O'er light divine by God's essence and presence;
Thus, seen through clouds
By aid He gives in secret,
The soul can, while on earth, enjoy His presence.

THE SOUL'S DESIRE TO BE WITH CHRIST

Del agua de la vida

I

FOR the living waters
My soul was seized with thirst insatiate,
    Yearning to quit
    This body and its ills,
And quaff of the eternal waters.

II

Fain doth it desire
To see itself delivered from these gyves,
  For life is tedious
  Dragged on in exile
From that dear fatherland of fond delight !

III

Its present pains increase
By numbering o'er the blessings it has lost ;
  And the heart breaks,
  Wounded by piercing pain,
Despoiled of the possession of its God.

IV

Happy that soul and blest
Which dwelleth ever present with its God !
  Aye, blest a thousandfold,
  For from a fount it drinks
Which to the end of time shall never fail !

V

True fatherland !
Thou solace of the souls that dwell in thee,
  Assuaging to the full !
  The just no longer weep
Within thy borders, but adore their God.

VI

Our earthly life,
Compared with thee, O never-ending life,
  Is so contemptible
  That we may truly say it is not life,
But death most burdensome !

VII

O Life curtailed and hard !
When shall I see myself despoiled of thee ?
O narrow sepulchre !
When will the Bridegroom for so long desired
Upraise me from thee ?

VIII

O God ! when shall I be
Wholly inflamed with Thy most sacred love ?
Alas, when dawns the day
That I may say farewell to things created
And be transported to Thee in Thy glory ?

IX

When, Love, O when ?
When comes the time I shall enjoy such bliss ?
When comes that ' when '
That I this dross
Forsake, and when such glorious victory ?

X

When shall I be united
To Thee, good Jesus, with a love so strong
That no incitement of the world,
The flesh, e'en death itself,
Nor eke the devil, can suffice
To break the unison ?

XI

When, O my God, shall I be set on fire
With Thy sweet love's enkindling ?
When shall I enter in at last to joy ?
Or when be offered
Wholly upon love's altar and consumed ?

XII

Oh that without delay
This loving love might all to ashes burn !
  Ah, when shall I attain
  To that most blessed state,
Never for all eternity to change again ?

XIII

My God, my only good,
My glory, and my comfort and my bliss,
  Withdraw me from this mire,
  This wretched earth,
To dwell in heaven with Thee for evermore !

XIV

Let me be one with Thee, my God,
Naught intervening, and withdraw Thou what impedes !
  Thaw Thou my coldness,
  Which doth now obstruct Thy love,
Curtailing its full measure !

XV

O that Thy love flamed with so fierce a glow
As to consume my heart !
  That it dissolved
  Or burnt me wholly
And struck from off my soul the body's yoke !

XVI

Ope, Lord, the portal of Thy love
To this poor wretch !
  Give certain hope
  Of everlasting love
To this weak, hapless worm of earth !

XVII

Delay Thou not to love
Nor to bestow a puissant love for Thee,
　Nor tarry Thou to turn Thine eyes on me,
　O God omnipotent,
Who stand for ever present in Thy sight !

XVIII

Thou bidd'st me call Thee,
And lo, I come with tears and cries to Thee !
　Thou bidd'st me love,
　And that is my desire !
But Thou, my Lord, till when ? O God ! till when,

XIX

Till when, wilt Thou delay to answer me ?
When give to me that love for which I crave ?
　Return and gaze on me—
　Behold I die—
And yet it seems Thou still dost fly from me.

XX

Ah, Lord eternal
My soul's delight, my glory.
　Ah, sempiternal Bounty,
　Day serene,
Thou Light, Thou Love, do not Thy grace postpone !

XXI

For Thee I'll sigh
While I am captive in this prison held !
　Ne'er will I stay,
　Recounting my petitions,
Until Thou hast raised up and crownèd me !

XXII

If I forget Thee,
My God, my sweetest Love, Who wooest me,
May I into oblivion dark sink down,
Nor of entire creation let there be
One who of me, sad soul, takes any thought!

ENTRÓ EL ALMA EN OLVIDO

Ecstasy

I

RAPT in oblivion, the soul
Doth, in a single moment, learn
More than the busy brain and sense,
With all their toil, could ever earn.

II

Mirrored within its God, it views
To-day, to-morrow, and the past,
And faith sees here, in *time*, the things
That through *eternity* shall last.

INDEX TO PASSAGES FROM HOLY SCRIPTURE

Roman figures refer to the Stanzas of the "Living Flame of Love"; P. to the "Instructions and Precautions"; L. to the Letters; M. to the "Spiritual Maxims."

311

INDEX

COSIMO is a specialty publisher of books and publications that inspire, inform and engage readers. Our mission is to offer unique books to niche audiences around the world.

COSIMO BOOKS publishes books and publications for innovative authors, non-profit organizations and businesses. **COSIMO BOOKS** specializes in bringing books back into print, publishing new books quickly and effectively, and making these publications available to readers around the world.

COSIMO CLASSICS offers a collection of distinctive titles by the great authors and thinkers throughout the ages. At **COSIMO CLASSICS** timeless classics find a new life as affordable books, covering a variety of subjects including: *Business, Economics, History, Personal Development, Philosophy, Religion and Spirituality,* and much more!

COSIMO REPORTS publishes public reports that affect your world: from global trends to the economy, and from health to geo-politics.

FOR MORE INFORMATION CONTACT US AT
INFO@COSIMOBOOKS.COM

✳ If you are a book-lover interested in our current catalog of books.

✳ If you are a bookstore, book club or anyone else interested in special discounts for bulk purchases

✳ If you are an author who wants to get published

✳ if you are an organization or business seeking to publish books and other publications for your members, donors or customers

COSIMO BOOKS ARE ALWAYS
AVAILABLE AT ONLINE BOOKSTORES

—————— VISIT COSIMOBOOKS.COM ——————
BE INSPIRED, BE INFORMED

CPSIA information can be obtained at www.ICGtesting.com
Printed in the USA
LVOW042326131011

250459LV00001B/63/A